THE 30 DAY GUIDE TO INNER PEACE

THE 30 DAY GUIDE TO INNER PEACE

JARED MADISON

Editor: Katherine Tandy Brown
Cover Art: Kanani Robinson

©The Innova Group LLC. Publishing Division

for Kathryn...

SPECIAL THANKS

Mom, thank you for being such an inspiration and positive example for me in this world. You have always sought to help cultivate my writing skills and as a result you "coaxed the brilliance out of slumbering genius." It is quite a blessing to have a mother that is on the same path as me spiritually, especially one that is as amazing as you are.

Kanani, thank you for being you. Thank you for your support, for your love, for your kindness, for your generosity, for being a best friend and partner. The road to manifesting your dreams can be challenging because most of the time, you only have this ideal that you're trying to bring to life, but you've always supported and believed in my vision; for that I am eternally grateful.

I would like to honor my father Richard Madison with this work. I am thankful that I have had a positive male role model, coach, and dad in you.

Special Thanks to Katherine Tandy Brown for being a motivator, mentor, teacher, and guide for me on this particular path.

INSTRUCTIONS FOR THIS GUIDEBOOK

It is important to meditate on each one of the daily practices and messages, therefore the most benefit will be gained by reading one chapter per day. To gain a more peaceful stance one must practice a more peaceful stance. In order to practice this stance, one must study the material presented within these pages intently, following the messages on a day-to-day basis. The more practice you have at being peaceful, the easier it will be to embody peace.

This guidebook and the practices and messages within were created purposefully as a natural progression towards deeper states of enlightenment. Reading multiple chapters per day would deduct from the power initiated through deeply contemplating the messages each day. In doing so, it may be of great benefit to sit with the messages of each chapter, truly incorporating the practice into your daily life, then viewing the effects of said practice before moving onto the next chapter.

Life gives us no shortage of experiences that may normally trigger an adverse reaction within us, however, you will now be given the tools to counteract your reactiveness; instead you will find yourself responding. If you consciously and consistently use the tools present within *The 30 Day Guide To Inner Peace,* you will first feel a change within you, then you will see that change manifest externally in your world and in your day to day activities.

If you treat this guidebook as if it were a course you decided to take on cultivating inner peace, your success is assured.

The 30 Day Guide To Inner Peace
By: Jared Madison

ON "GOD"

Not until the review and editing process of this book did I realize how often I used the word "God." As human consciousness evolves into higher degrees of evolutionary expansion, many people may perhaps synonymize this particular word with aversion and denial. This may be in part due to the convoluted spiritual "truths" passed down by religious institutions as a perceived means of control as well as the disgruntled disposition of the patriarchal God portrayed in the Old Testament of the King James Bible. I beseech of those of you who hold apprehension towards the word God not to let seeing this name deter you from the truths presented within these following pages.

Contrarily, there are those among us who cling tightly to the word God, highlighting their adamant respect, and adulation for their supreme deity. Being brought up to worship and praise God through more traditional methodologies however, does not take away from the potency of this intricate concept. Even in the darkest of rooms a small candle may still exude light. I ask those of you not to shy away from this work when you hear me refer to, "God" by other names; "A rose by any other name..."

I would also like to acknowledge those readers who may not believe in God at all. In my opinion these individuals perhaps have the greatest potential for an expedited spiritual transformation. The skeptic's revelation, when reached, correlates to an experienced personal perspicuity, one that can not be inculcated. We all must come to know ourselves as

God. This is something that we cannot be convinced of, it is something that must be experienced. I implore those of you not to allow God to dissuade you from these instructions on how to cultivate peace. There is a quite epic intelligence that runs through all of creation. Give it whatever name you will or no name at all, but trust that there is an energy in-between atoms that hold all of matter together; I am discussing the void that gives rise to this energy.

All this is to say, we mustn't get caught up in the mundane details. Words are secondary to sound. Sound is secondary to vibration. It is in this place below all other places that this word, whether it be Universe, Spirit, or God, truly dwells. Your idea of God should infinitely evolve, or rather devolve, into unexplainable seeming nothingness, if you wish to seek the truth. It is when we give something a name that we take away its power. When we say a thing is, "over there", we diminish its ability to be "over here."

In your search for ultimate truth, remember to continually go deeper.

Give yourself permission for your idea about God and Her name to change. You will see me use the word "Uni" to describe my idea of God throughout this guidebook. At the time of this book's inception, Uni was a name I loving held onto to call upon God; today that has changed. My current descriptive belief in God most closely aligns with the description of The Dao in *Tao Te Ching* by Lao Tzu:

"The Dao that can be told
is not the eternal Dao
The name that can be named
Is not the eternal Name
The unnamable is the eternally real

Naming is the origin of all things
Free from desire, you realize the
mystery
Caught in desire, you see only the
manifestations
Yet mystery and manifestations
arise from the same source
This source is called darkness
Darkness within darkness
The gateway to all understanding"

My dear friend, clear and open your mind…
to become a master, meet each day as a student.

ON MEDITATION

"How can just sitting there and thinking of nothing really have an affect on my wellbeing?" This was my first question in regards to the benefits of meditation. From my perspective I saw that the whole world was about action and doing, getting up and clocking in, building, producing, cultivating, achieving. How could "nothing" produce "something"? Nonetheless, I was reminded time and time again through seemingly every spiritual work I read that a well maintained meditation practice was the key to spiritual, physical, and emotional transformation and opulence.

It was said that Siddhartha Gautama (also know as the Buddha) meditated for seven days straight beneath a fig tree without food or water. There are historical references that point to Isa (sanskrit for Lord later known as Jesus in the Bible), spending a significant amount of his youth in India studying yoga mediation. These two men have significantly shaped the course of human consciousness as well as our incorporeal gestation. This being the case, if I wanted to even dream of becoming a spiritual teacher in my own right, meditation was something I had to look deeper into on my journey.

I reluctantly began my meditation practice five minutes at a time. Eventually, five minutes turned into 10, 10 minutes turned into 15 and so on until I reached my personal record of 2 hours in meditation. During this process I realized why all those books I had read talked about the importance of meditation, and why Jesus and Buddha studied this esoteric art-it cleared an internal pathway to the Divine.

Within this guidebook I discuss meditation on many different occasions in reference to positively cultivating a serene state of inner peace. It came to my understanding that perhaps, some people may not be as well versed in this particular subject matter as others. Therefore, I will briefly discuss what "meditation" means to me as well as how a beginner can start a practice of his/her own.

Setting The Mood:

- Deeper states of meditation can be reached when you have a specific set amount of time that you can delegate to undisturbed solitude and quietness.
- Meditation music can be helpful, as it soothes the mind into a relaxed state. You can YouTube, "meditation music" and find something that resonates with you.
- Sitting upright in a comfortable chair is recommended to improve focus. If you are lying down and you're like me at all, you'll fall asleep by accident.
- Lighting candles and incense can create a sacred space. It is not necessary but it might assist you in your process. Whatever you can do to make your meditation practice sanctified, the greater benefit you will receive; rituals correlate to habits, habits correlate to consistency.

The Focus:

- The key to meditation is the breath. I have learned that when you begin any practice, you need to give the mind something to focus on. So meditation is not simply about "doing nothing", it is about focusing on the breath.

- When your mind begins to run wild with thoughts about your day, about your past, about your future, gently return your focus to your breath.
- It's perfectly normal for the mind to think, the mind is just being the mind. You are beyond your mind and as you begin to consciously turn your focus inward to your breath, you will begin to see yourself as the observer.

The Silent Observer:

- As you continue to come back to the breath, you will start to begin to witness your thoughts. They seemingly rise and fall like the ocean waves. You can acknowledge your thoughts but it is key not to entertain them.
- Imagine you are sitting on your porch and there are people, animals, and things from all walks of life that are walking down the street in front of your house. Some things may be interesting and captivating; however, your job is to just sit on your porch and allow the passers by to...pass by.
- Begin to feel and realize that there exists a part of you, non-physical, that is observing life happen apathetically.
- Watch your thoughts come and go.

Instructions for Meditation:

1. Find a quiet place to sit where you can be undisturbed for five minutes.
2. Light any candles or incense and find some meditation music you might like. This is not required, however it may help.
3. Sit down and set your timer for five minutes. You can of course go longer if you like.

4. Close your eyes and begin to focus all your attention on your breath.

5. Inhale as deeply as you can...pause at the top of your breath....then exhale as gently as you can. With your inhale, fill your lungs with as much oxygen as possible. With your exhale, try to empty all of the oxygen out of your lungs.

6. Focus on the feeling and action of life itself entering and exiting your body.

7. Begin by focusing on your toes and move all the way up to your head, relaxing each part of your body that you focus on.

The purpose of meditation is not to get you anywhere but to remind you that you are in fact everywhere and you possess everything. Our mind can cast a thick fog over our internal recognition of one-ness with Spirit.

Imagine that you have all the answers that you will ever need, but they are inside a glass jar with sand and water. The mind as it stirs, and flips, and turns, causes the water inside the jar to mix with the sand and become murky; therefore, the answers are hidden so much so that you forget you have them. Meditation simply rests the glass jar on a table and allows for the sand and water to separate, revealing what was previously hidden.

Everything has to become about what's going on inside of you, your beliefs, your disposition, your thoughts, and your feelings. You will see the external world reflected through the eyes of this internal onlooker. Your success therefore will depend on your perception, the practice of meditation will help clarify your vision...

AN INTRODUCTION TO PEACE

Standing in my friend's garden one day, surrounded by Buddhist yard statues, I found myself in a state of hypnotized wonderment, questioning the reason why it seemed as if all the statues of Buddha were carved in stone or made to look as if they were carved from stone. I came to understand that the reason for this was that stone is immovable and the Buddha represented peace itself, therefore the statues were carved in stone as to represent immovable peace. In the same moment I came to this enlightening realization, I also had the desire to reach this place which these statues so effortlessly portrayed.

How does one reach a state in which no matter what the outer conditions demonstrate the inner resonance stays the same? *The 30 Day Guide To Inner Peace* is the answer to this question. This is my trail journal on my personal path to become a stone statue of peace. I asked Uni (my name for God, short for The Universe) how I could possibly accomplish moving this mountain of mountains and She responded with the 30 lessons presented within this guidebook. I have walked this path, and now I find myself continually at the destination I so adamantly sought.

One of the coolest things about embarking on this journey to a place of immovable inner peace is that you will begin to see the tangibility of God play out in your life; as you reap so shall you sow. As you do the work, you will see the results. You will become a blessing to all around you by the simple act of being.

Welcome to *The 30 Day Guide To Inner Peace*, and may the Force be with you...

TABLE OF CONTENTS

Day 1

WILL THIS BRING ME
CLOSER TO INNER
PEACE?

As you flow through life and are challenged to remain centered in the midst of turbulent circumstances, you can ask yourself, "Will this thought, word, action, or decision bring me closer to a state of inner peace?" If the answer is "no" and you still decide to move forward, you are consciously acknowledging the fact that you are deviating from your ultimate objective. If you wish to reach a place of inner peace and you understand said action will lead you in the opposite direction of your goal and you proceed anyway, you are willingly sabotaging your-self. To pause before reacting gives you the space to consciously choose the next step of your journey. You will either take a step closer to a place of eternal peace or you will take a step further away.

The "willing sabotage" discussed in the previous paragraph can take on a positive resonance. Once you pose the question, "Will this bring me closer to a state of inner peace?" you have at once negated the quite natural human tendency to react, by first pausing. This is a precious moment because it is from this place of pausing that you can make a more sensible decision. More than likely if the answer is "no", you will choose a new decision that will lead you closer to a state of inner peace. The usefulness of the "willing sabotage" comes from the experience of pain/suffering endured as a result of making a decision from a point of fear, pain, anger, frustration, anxiety, etc. that takes you in the opposite direction of your goal. A negative reinforcement works well in this case because when the next opportunity arises and the question is again posed, you will ponder the question while remembering what happened the last time you willingly chose to "go the wrong way".

This question from the Day 1 practice is a wonderful tool, especially in the case of our thoughts. Many times, it may seem as if we have very little control over our thoughts; some seem to rise and fall like the waves from some unbeknown ocean of an abyss. At times those thoughts can be negative in nature and can create fear, sadness, anxiety, or depression in the body. Countering the negative thought with a positive thought can be strenuous, especially during a period of sadness, worry, or depression. The question, "Will this thought bring me closer to inner peace?" is less trying, as it asks the mind to make a clear-cut decision that will benefit the overall health of the whole organism, aka YOU. If you can create a positive relationship in the mind between thinking good thoughts and feeling good, you can trick the mind into habitually moving closer to your destination of peace.

Throughout your day today, when you encounter internal thoughts, or situations and experiences that usually cause you to react, pause and ask yourself, "Will this thought, word, or action bring me closer to my desired destination of inner peace?" Then make your informed decision.

Day 2

HOW HAS WORRYING
HELPED ME?

In the past, when faced with a challenging situation, has worrying ever led you to a brilliant solution? What gifts have you received from the downward-spiraling thoughts produced by worry? Thus far have you been able to manufacture peace from uneasiness? With the Day 2 practice you will begin to eradicate the things which no longer serve your highest purpose, worry being one of the cardinal issues.

Planning is a very beneficial and effective way to reach a desired outcome. Worry, however, has nothing to do with planning; the energies are in opposition of one another. Planning requires calculation and forethought while in a serene state of mind. When planning anything, the planner usually envisions the most favorable and efficient route to a desired point. Planning is usually done over the course of time so that the best possible outcome may be achieved.

When I think of worry, the image of someone flamboyantly flapping around in the middle of the ocean trying not to drown enters my mind.

What logical response can someone have during an experience of seeming demise as endorphins saturated with fear flood the bloodstream?

Synonymous with torment and distress, worry will not help you reach a place of immovable inner peace. Worry comes in the form of anxious thoughts. Your most fearful thoughts are *not* your reality. When we worry, we play "make believe" and as the all-mighty and wise adults we proclaim ourselves to be, we proceed to act in accordance with the "make believe" world we have created. In the case of being consumed with worrisome and anxious thoughts, how can we logically expect the imaginary to yield the actual?

Nine out of ten times the worst-case scenario will never come to pass. In the case of worrying we are literally killing ourselves over nothing; worrying releases adrenaline, spikes blood pressure, and can even alter the natural rhythm of the heart. When we worry, we trigger the sympathetic nervous system into fight or flight mode as the body's natural response to hopefully keep us alive from imminent death. In terms of worrying, we have convinced the loving vessel called the body that there is something on the immediate horizon that will surely kill us, and we need to take immediate evasive action in order to avoid our instantaneous dissolution. Imagine the effect constant worry has on your health over a long period of time, when the body constantly believes you are in danger.

The Tools:

The rebuttal to worry's profoundly enlightened arguments is God. Your work when faced with a worrisome situation is to do the absolute most and best that you can to facilitate your desired outcome of peace. The remainder you leave in the loving hands of The Universe to sort out.

I have had my fair share of interactions with anxiety and worry, but over time I developed tools (with assistance from Uni) that have helped me manage and overcome the fears at the center of my worries.

Here is my thought process when engaged with a fear and/or worry:

****Fearful thing is on the horizon**...
(insert ominous music)**

1. Do I believe that The Universe is all loving?

• Yes

2. Do I believe that I have a very special and intimate relationship with The Universe?

• Yes, of course, I even call her Uni. We are best friends.

3. Do I believe that this all-encompassing, omnipresent force is not with me in this situation?

• I cannot believe that Uni is omnipresent (everywhere) and also believe that She is not here. Even though it may look and feel as if I am alone, I know based upon my belief and my previous experiences of God, that She is here as well.

4. If I believe God is all encompassing, all loving, and He is my best-friend, and I also believe that He loves me unconditionally and is right here with me during this trouble, how could God forsake me and allow something to happen to me that wouldn't benefit my overall evolution or good?

- I don't believe God would forsake me. In the past when I have felt afraid during/after something "bad" happened, even when I was in the absolute wrong, something always happened beyond my control that swayed the outcome in my favor. When things could have gone wrong for me, I was spared the rod of "worst case scenario."

5. I have worried frantically about things in the past just so things would ultimately turn out fine to the point where it has affected my health. I have had panic attacks, insomnia and even high blood pressure as a result of worrying, yet the apocalyptic scenario I had conjured up with my child-like imagination had never come to pass. Despite my dramatic propagations to The Universe, things have always turned out far better than I dreadfully expected.

- Worrying is a waste of my time and energy. It isn't good for my body, and I love my body! I also love being happy and at peace. So, "Uni I am worried about________. I know you are with me, but I still feel alone, and I still have some doubt. I would like your help dealing with this issue. Please allow me to see through your eyes and to see this as the blessing I believe it must be..."

*****END EXAMPLE*****

At the end of my internal examination, I come to the point where I can openly and honestly make a request to The Universe for assistance, not the deliverance from a situation, not to be rescued, but to see the truth. If I can observe the lesson in the situation, then I can immediately begin to do the work. The miracle happens as a result of my willingness to do the work. The Universe is in a constant state of "this is a teaching moment" with us. Some of us require a harsher molding of our souls into godliness. Others of us can, "catch God on the whisper." Having this perspective has changed my life in a very positive way because it has allowed me to come to an understanding that everything I experience is a blessing from God. What else other than love would God be able to give, if God is all encompassing, infinitely expanding love?

Of course, I still feel the feelings of worry, but I do not allow those feelings to consume me. I do not allow those fearful thoughts associated with worry to saturate my mind. By posing a series of internal questions, I can begin to identify the fear that is at the root of my anxious thoughts. When I reach this place, I can begin to heal from within and allow the miracle to manifest without.

Next time you are faced with a challenging situation, try starting a journal. Be as open and honest as you can with your entries. Make note of the date, time, and all your feelings associated with the situation. Sit in a meditative state and talk to The Universe, letting Her know how you feel. Ask for God's assistance in seeing the challenge you find your-self in from His magical perspective, all the while allowing yourself to truly feel the doubt, fear, or worry.

Continue journaling throughout the duration of your challenge, making note of the day and time when it has passed. Put your journal away for one month or so in a safe place without looking at it. After roughly 30 days has passed, re-read your journal entries. Notice how you were feeling at the time, all the while keeping in mind the way in which the situation was resolved.

This journaling exercise is a wonderful tool and can be done with each seeming catastrophe you face in your life. As you take note of your feelings, as well as how each event turned out, you will start to compile the evidence that proves to your incessant mind that, "every little thing will be okay." When you go back and re-read past entries and fearful instances, you will have to acknowledge that event "X" was way "worse" than this current catastrophe, and everything still turned out okay. When you become consciously aware that things have always turned out at least okay for you, you will be able to live a more peaceful existence.

Day 3

DEVELOPING
A PERSONAL
RELATIONSHIP WITH
GOD

Society does quite a wonderful job of telling us how the world works and what is expected of us from an early age on. This goes for who and what God is as well. Our religious/spiritual perspective therefore depends a great deal on the geographic location of our birth, as well as the religious/spiritual views of the group of people we call our community. In this case, it is most likely expected and even comfortable to simply believe what everyone else around us believes. There is no work or challenge here. The mind rests in a state of comfortable ease; All That Is can fit simply into a small box. But does such a confined idea of God work for such a liberated concept?

Everything in our perceivable Universe is energy in motion and like the different colors that make up the rainbow, you are unique and there is no other soul/energy/color quite like you. You flow through life with your own unique experiences, as well as triumphs and challenges. No other being in all the galaxies, in all of creation sees things exactly the way you do. Because you are the only one having your particular experience of life, you will have different fears, different dreams, and different needs than others.

Let's say that all of creation is one very big, very magnificent mountain and the goal of creation is to reach the top of this mountain. We each start at a different place at the bottom of the mountain in a 360-degree circle around the base. An infinite number of paths lead to the top. Earlier on in life you may feel as if you are on an expedition with a large group of people (family, friends, and community) but somewhere on your path to the top, you start to feel a pull towards a different path.

This pull feels weird at first, almost wrong, because as you relay your feelings to your closest allies, you are met with staunch opposition. "This is the way that we have always traveled. This is the path my parents, and their parents, have traveled." Meagerly, you fall back in line to continue the well-traveled path. Time passes and you feel this pull again, this time so much so that you decide to, against all advice, seek your own path to the mountaintop.

Your new path seems easy at first due to the euphoric liberation that initially courses through your veins like the waters of the rapids; you've gotten your first taste of true freedom. Yet as time goes on, you become frightened with anxiety-soaked thoughts as things become increasingly more challenging. During this new, challenging and anxiety soaked segment of your journey safety in the comfort of numbers, as well as always being able to see what lies ahead, begins to appeal to you more and more. But it is in this place of uncomfortable vexation that you will begin to cultivate a personal relationship with God, simply because you are seemingly alone on this new path and a powerful, almighty friend wouldn't be such a bad comrade on your journey.

Going off the preceding example, your relationship with God will be unique to your personal experiences on your trail because your path, for example, may take you through thick brush. Therefore, you may pray for a machete, while the path you left your family on was much smoother, ergo sharp tools were not required to clear the way. Perhaps another person who sought his own path to the mountaintop experiences snowstorms on his path, so he prays for warmer clothes. Another person on her path must traverse rivers, so she prays for supplies to build a boat.

Due to a biological, as well as spiritual, tendency towards progress, you will one day find yourself on a quest to the mountaintop (if you're not already on it) because your soul yearns for the adventure of really finding out what it's made of. If you were in fact made in the image of The Creator, and The Creator is infinitely expansive, this means that you are inherently, infinitely expansive. The way others have gone doesn't quite seem to fit you, and that's perfectly fine. When you have gathered your belongings and have set out on your own journey, you will find that God communicates with you differently than He does with anyone else.

My personal relationship with Uni is wonderful. I am able to be myself, openly and honestly; most importantly, I am always in communication with Her. My God is feminine most of the time. She reminds me of my grandmother. However, His energy does change. He communicates with me through symbolism quite often; I'm a visual learner, so I am able to quickly identify instances of "What's up?" "How are you!?", from God through the signs He sends me.

When it comes to Uni, "fear" is not a word I would use when discussing our relationship. I love Her deeply and I know there is no condition in which Uni's love for me is tied. I believe Uni understands *(perhaps due to experience, but let's not go too deep down the rabbit hole)* that the human experience is vastly challenging. As such, I liken myself to a baby learning how to walk, whereas Uni is a loving parent guiding me through the process. Loving parents never demean their children for falling when they are learning how to walk; the energy of "support" is the quite natural response. I also have come to understand and believe that Uni knows my heart so well that He recognizes I am trying my best. I have cultivated my extensive relationship with God over the course of my entire life to this point, and it continues to evolve.

The Day 3 practice asks that you start to cultivate your very own personal relationship with God. The easiest way to do this is by first getting into a quiet meditative state. Once this is accomplished, you can begin an open and honest dialogue with God. An example of an icebreaker would go something like, "I want to see evidence of your presence at work in my life; I ask that you show me signs that you are with me..." After you have finished your preamble, get ready for the fireworks display! It seems like The Universe is waiting on pins and needles for us to seek out a genuine relationship with It.

Tip: Being present in the moment also helps when cultivating a personal relationship with God. I have learned that God communicates subtly most of the time, therefore presence in each moment is essential. The name of the game is awareness.

Start to look for God in the places where you feel the most comfortable and at peace. The place where I can easily rendezvous with The Divine is nature. I have had so many profound "aha" moments by simply walking in nature with a full awareness of the present moment. As a matter of fact, the most intriguing analogies that I have correlated to life/reality and The Universe have come from nature.

Begin the next moment by asking God the easiest way the two of you can open a loving and continuous dialogue, then listen intently. Your answers are on the way.

Day 4

WHERE CAN I BREATHE?

This is the question you can pose to all your anxious, fearful and/or worrisome thoughts. To pause and ask yourself, "Where can I breathe?" in the middle of a difficult situation is a tremendous act of grace and trust.

If you can only breathe in the present, unable to breathe in the past or in the future, and if you are "okay" in the present, you are therefore infinitely "okay". Whatever it is that is seeking to destroy you must do so when you are alive, and you can only be alive when you are breathing. Thus, if an attack must come from somewhere, it must come in the now, thereby each successful breath reverberates peace.

Countless outcomes may become your reality in the next instant. You only have the ability to imagine some of these future outcomes and the mind will more than likely gravitate towards the worst-case scenario examples if fear is involved. When the mind confronts you with these troubling realities ask yourself another question, "What is going on right now?" The body's constant response to this question will be, "breathing..."

A Practice for Peace:

- *Breathe in: feel the air enter your lungs, sending loving light and energy to all the cells in your body; this action gives life to your being.*
- *Breathe out: feel your entire vessel release, allowing each cell to alleviate itself from what no longer serves it. Feel your chest expand and then contract. This is life is. This act of movement in the unmoving is God.*

If by your simple act of breathing, you are a miracle manifested, what do you think your entire existence reflects? You are much larger than your problems, or the circumstances of your life. If you were never born, then whatever hardship you are facing right now or in the future would not exist. All the people you may interact with as a result of this current or future challenge would not be having this experience as well, if you did not exist. In fact, you are the reason for this moment because if you were not here in this moment, then this moment would not exist. You are the cause of all of this.

This moment is passing; you are eternal. You *will* learn and grow from all your challenges; you *will* evolve while the challenging circumstances fade away into oblivion. That which once caused such tremendous pain will be transformed into a scar; wisdom heals. Do you think that anything was created to destroy you? More importantly, do you think there is anything in existence that God does not have the power to heal instantaneously?

Wherever you are, whatever you are doing, whatever you are facing, all the aspects of this experience are there because you are the focal point holding them together and wherever you find yourself, you will also find God.

The Day 4 Practice asks that as you face your next instance of overthinking, ask yourself, "Where can I breathe?" then answer the request of the only place where you can be alive...the now. Remember to be gentle with yourself. Most of us have had a lifetime of allowing the mind and anxious thoughts to call the shots, therefore we may be met with firm resistance as we reclaim our powerful presence and peace of mind.

Day 5

WHAT IS BEING ASKED OF ME RIGHT NOW?

...and what is your answer? In this moment, what would you say The Universe is asking of you? Perhaps it is to simply sit here and read this book. Perhaps your child has just come up to you asking for attention. Maybe your stomach has signaled to you that it's time for a snack.

Whether you're in your car, in line at the supermarket, in class, or at work, you can ask yourself, "What is being asked of me right now?", whenever you start to feel impatient, anxious, angry, frustrated, or any other emotion you do not enjoy experiencing. Quite often, the answer to this question is simply, "to be present".

A state of conscious presence is still the aim, even when someone is being particularly unpleasant to you. Perhaps in this case the person just needs someone to listen to them; perhaps they are frustrated with other aspects of their own life that they cannot control and need an outlet to alleviate the internal pressure they feel.

Conscious presence, even in the face of obnoxiousness is a wonderful opportunity to practice non-reactiveness. If you feel "attacked" but you can still pause and pose a question, then you can immediately transform a tumultuous situation into a blessing. Here again, the act of pausing is illustrated as a power tool for spiritual evolution.

We cannot control the outside world, but we do have some control over our thoughts and even more control over our actions. An unyielding state of inner peace equates to the understanding that the world will not be loving, kind, or fair to us 100% of the time. Instead, we have simply decided to believe that we are loved, safe, and smiled upon in every situation no matter what may appear to be presented on the surface. Defense is a natural reaction to threat, but what can someone truly take away from you? Peace is a true reflection of strength as the understanding has been reached that if God is inclusive, nothing can truly be harmed or threatened because everything is truly One Thing.

We all have bills that need to be paid, and trials to be triumphed over. However, we will negate the full strength of our power in any given situation by attempting to create outside this moment. We can plan for tomorrow, today, but if Life is asking for our patience right now and we are giving our franticness, then we will experience this discord as challenge and a seeming deviation from our well-being.

Let's break down what "Universe" means exactly.

Uni-*prefix*

Definition of *uni-*

:one : single

Verse-*noun*

Definition of *verse-*

1 : a line of metrical writing

metrical writing- "written in the form of poetry, with a pattern of strong and weak beats." ~idoceonline.com

We can thereby summarize that "Universe" means, one singular beat or rhythm. Therefore, The Universe singularly vibrates with the essence of peace, meaning any other vibration/tempo that we may find ourselves on, isn't God, which would therefore make us feel "off-beat" or anxious, or pessimistic, or worried. Have you ever seen someone dancing or clapping off-beat? It doesn't look or feel right, does it? Use this as an example the next time someone or something derails you temporarily from dancing with God.

Let me reiterate the act of pausing when faced with any situation where strong emotions are present. To pause and pose a question expounds your power and magnifies it tenfold. I use this same question from The Day 5 Practice, *"What is being asked of me right now?"*, in my meditation practice and in the world whenever I feel myself overthinking, trying to figure out how to solve all the problems of tomorrow, right now. The cool thing about this is that as soon as I pause and "chill out", the answers to my inquiries are seemingly beamed to me as if from some Universal Mothership. Remember, as you experience fear, worry, or overthinking, pause and ask yourself, "What is being asked of me right now?"

When you are able to surrender to the moment a bit, you will allow everything to come to you when you need it; by letting go, you attract. This is meditation in motion.

Day 6

JUDGE NOT

Judgment is expecting perfection from another while at the same time being imperfect. If we couple in the fact that "perfection" will be defined differently by each individual, it is easily demonstrated that being judgmental is a faulty outlook based upon false pretenses. In that case, where is the sensibility or fairness regarding judgment? If we continually search from insensibility and unfairness in the world, what is it that we will find?

Space and therefore time will be experienced by each of us differently because we each have our own, very unique "place" from where we stand and perceive reality. Two people can be standing side by side, while viewing the same painting and see two totally different images because of the angles at which light reflects off the painting and back to their eyes. Using this example, is someone "wrong" because the image they see is different from yours?

Lovingly allowing others to have a vastly different perception of reality than you do, while they stand right next to you can be extremely challenging. The true question to ask yourself in this case is, "Why does this person's perception of reality upset me?" As you search the depths of your soul for the answer, it is likely that you will find that this "judgment" is being fueled by fear. Correlating this example to the realm of different religious ideologies, judgment of others' beliefs may be a result of a grave fear that if "they" are right, then I am "wrong", and if I am wrong then I will certainly be denied salvation. Or perhaps you may believe that their "wrong-ness" is the reason why the world is in the shape that it is in. Just as you hold your "belief" as absolute truth and seemingly have the evidence and backing to affirm this truth, the other has his/her evidence and backing as well. In this case, the trophy ordained to the winning party is a stalemate. And should we aim to win stagnation on the path of spiritual evolution?

Lovingly allowing someone to perceive reality from their vantage point without judgment can heal the world in an instant. We each see the world differently and that's okay because we are all held by the most loving, most miraculous, most forgiving energy there is...God! So it was, it is, and it will be all okay no matter how things may appear.

The Day 6 Practice may be one of the most challenging exercises because of the habitual nature that we have acquired in reference to judgment. It seems easier in the human experience to point to others lack of, than it is to resolve our own inequities. If you find yourself consciously seeking higher realms of reality, what good will it do you to pause your evolution in order to make a negative presumption of another? Even if you consider your daily endeavors to be totally virtuous, there will always be at least one person who will look upon your actions with aversion. A quite wonderful example of this would be that of the life of Yeshua of Judea (Jesus). Judgment holds no value at all and if you wish to increase your frequency, how would you do so by adding nothing at all?

The surrender of judgment in any case will surely lighten your load and allow for a swifter ascension towards the ever-expanding heavenly realities that increased enlightenment yields. I, however, implore you not to change your judgemental perspective as a result of fear, due to some karmic debt that you will incur as a result of judgment or some punishment from an angry God because you were judgy. Instead, cease the judgment of the world because it does nothing for you.

You may be saying to yourself, "But what about using judgment as a means of keeping safe?" Intuition is my response. That "gut feeling" we all experience when the soul knows instinctively that something is out of sorts should be relied upon rather than judgment, which can come from the insane suggestion of a customarily fearful ego. Intuition is a deep knowing, whereas judgment is a speculative suggestion. We all possess the natural senses to keep us from harm's way, and intuition is this sixth sense.

We have all been a victim of judgment and we know that it doesn't feel very good. Knowing how it feels to be judged, imagine now that you are giving that feeling knowingly and willingly to everyone you judge. Instead of giving love, compassion, or understanding; you are **choosing** to give condemnation. If you would like to live a life filled with more happiness, more love, and of course, more peace, how can you accomplish this if what you are continually giving is in opposition to the energy of your desired destination? How do you hope to reach a place of inner peace if you keep taking steps towards separation?

If you consciously or unconsciously seek denial (denial and judgment being synonymous), then you consciously or unconsciously create denial. Denial is the byproduct of judgment. If you consciously seek peace, then you will consciously create peace. Serenity is the byproduct of peace. From a higher perspective there may be no real "right" or "wrong"; instead, it may be a simply a matter of "doing this" or "doing that" which gets you "here" or "there". In this example, judgment simply takes us elsewhere than a place of inner peace.

Whenever an opportunity arises that would normally trigger judgment, ask yourself,
"Will this perception bring me closer to a state of inner peace?"

Day 7

RADICAL ACCEPTANCE

Like most spiritual practices, the art of radical acceptance is much easier said than done. How do you accept something when you are in total disagreement with it? More so, will that acceptance mean that the circumstances surrounding the situation be justified?

If it's going, let it go, and if it's coming, let it in. The most perfectly constructed arena to practice radical acceptance is when you are "here", and you want so desperately to be "over there". No amount of yearning or exertion ever made a butterfly out of a caterpillar. The transformative process to butterfly-ness is happening all of the caterpillar's life; every second a metamorphosis is taking place. It is simply at one occurrence that we see this particular flower blossom.

Okay, so if it's happening all the time—"happening", meaning your continual evolution towards a destination of infinite happiness and abundant opulence—then that means it's happening even when it appears that nothing is happening at all. The growth process of a baby is a perfect example. It seems that if you take your eyes off a newborn for too long, you will find a teenager in its place. The reason why babies seem to grow so fast is due to the rate at which their cells are dividing. Humans are made up of trillions of cells, and as these cells divide, new tissue is formed; bones stretch, organs propagate, and muscles strengthen. Human males tend to stop growing at the age of 18 on average. So, from birth to 18 years old, the human male will continually grow all day, every day. This means that their bodies are literally moving all day, every day. Since the individual units (the cells) that make up the total entity (the body) are in constant motion, it is therefore impossible for the body to be "stuck". All this is to say, life is a process of continual evolution and continual movement. Since you are a part of life, your experiences of life are also in a state of perpetual motion.

Everything in our observable Universe is made up of energy/light and light/energy travels via waves. Waves all have a trough (the lowest point) and a crest (the highest point). The natural motion of life is therefore cyclical as creation itself is one big ebb and flow. The first law of thermodynamics, also known as the Law of Conservation of Energy, states that energy can neither be created nor destroyed; energy can only be transferred or changed from one form to another. Since energy cannot be destroyed, the transfer of energy is infinitely occurring. Since you are made of atoms, you are made of energy, since you are made of energy, you are made of light. Because you are made of light, you are in a state of constant motion; your body is literally vibrating right now even though it may seem as if you are sitting perfectly still.

***

"There is neither birth nor death, only successive manifestations"
~Thich Nhat Hanh

***

In order to really be "stuck", you must defy the laws of physics. How much easier does it now seem to accept something disagreeable, now that you are aware that change is the at the basis of all creation? Even when things appear to be chaotic, or perhaps at a standstill/low-point, you are ultimately moving to a place of more peace/love/happiness/joy, all the while gaining a tremendous amount of wisdom through the process. During troubling times, I would always remind myself with a silent affirmation,

"troughs and crests/ high's and low's"

More than likely, you view your reality from the perspective of being "here" and then moving to "there"; however, the truth is that this movement to "there" is eternally happening. Right now, you are moving to a new height in life. But, we all need a little faith in order to "sit on our hands", allowing the process to naturally evolve. One of the good things about The Universe is that things are always getting better, and because you are a part of All of This, your life and experiences will also, always be getting better.

Affirmation: "In each and every day, in each and every way, my life is getting better and better."

One of the biggest apprehensions that comes into play regarding this "allowing" reflects a false truth that we hold in reverence, due to the capitalistic teachings of the belief that hard work is the only path to success. Perhaps more importantly, coming forth in all endeavors with an ideology that accepts force (hard work) as the means to attain success, will reinforce the need to be in total control of each and every situation, especially those in which a particular ideal is attempting to be realized. Force constricts, peace relaxes. If The Universe itself is flow, what would be the result of constricting our vessels/straining to obtain a goal?

The energy of allowing is in total opposition to that of hard work in its traditional respect. Your personal relationship with The Universe comes into play here because you will have to take a more trusting approach to this "allowing" as you understand that you have a specifically unique role to play out with your existence. Wherever it is that you truly want to be, you will one day find yourself; however, it may not look exactly the same as you had envisioned; nevertheless it will *feel* exactly how you imagined it would feel.

The role that you play is different from any other soul in the entire Universe; no one else can do your job! For example, cells have vastly different jobs and the animals on our planet play out different roles. An example of "hard work" would be a white blood cell trying to do the job of a red blood cell, or a honeybee trying to do the job of an ant. Regarding working on this book, I would say that I am in a creative flow with The Universe; I don't consider this to be "hard work". I find this to be an act of loving creation, challenging at times but always rewarding. You will find that trying to do the job of another soul is "hard work"; however, when you find your true purpose in life, it will be totally fulfilling.

I have had jobs where I have had to work hard because those occupations went against the yearning desires of my soul. On the road to where I am now, I would become frustrated and discouraged because I wasn't living the life I knew I was meant to live. I would find myself in careers/jobs that paid the bills but failed to enhance my spiritual advancement; that was hard work.

Hard work is being fully immersed in a career that you do not love simply for financial gain and security. In the search for inner peace, I recommend finding a career/job that has some aspects that truly make your heart sing, while you continually nurture your highest dreams in your spare time. Maybe you are a people-person, and you are good at giving advice filled with sagely wisdom. In this example, something like customer service may suit you quite well. It may not be your dream job, however if you are able to constantly seek opportunities in the mundane, the mundane will be transformed into the extraordinary.

Do your work. Follow your dreams. Use the internal GPS of the heart. In all that you seek to acquire, *feel* your way there. See if you can feel the difference between going upriver and going with the current. See how things may seemingly fall into place in one instance and how roadblock after roadblock may keep coming up in another. Accept where you are currently, while setting a gentle intention to be wherever you wish to be. In this case, if it goes, let it go, and if it comes, let it in. If it feels like you're stuck in a rut, take a nap. If it feels like you've started moving in a certain direction, even if that direction doesn't quite look like what you've envisioned as your dream, go with it, see where it takes you. The vision we have for our highest good is almost never what specifically manifests in our life due to our limited perspective of our reality.

Would you rather The Universe with its vastly omnipresent and infinitely expansive perspective assist you in reaching a place of total abundant fulfillment and love, or would you rather choose to reach whatever destination your limited mind could conjure up? Would you rather use God's mind or your own when it comes to manifesting the best possible reality for yourself?

The Day 7 Practice asks that you take a nap whenever you feel stuck. Taking a nap is both a literal and figurative means to assist you in reaching a place of inner peace. Taking a nap simply involves letting go, accepting, and getting comfortable with the seeming non-movement you're experiencing. In my particular experience of life, whenever I am experiencing an ebb (low point), it usually means that things are about to pick up in a major way. Therefore, I recognize those periods and I am able to rest accordingly as well as do any necessary spiritual maintenance for the road ahead.

Accept your experience of life fully when nothing seems to be moving, all the while remembering that things are always moving; this will surely enhance the presence of peace in both your internal and external worlds. If you start to feel doors opening in a totally different direction than you previously envisioned, curiously go with the flow. You might just end up exactly where you wanted to be, or perhaps even somewhere better.

Day 8

THE PROCLAMATION: "WHO ARE YOU?"

A state of immovable inner peace requires the conscious awareness and classification of one's self.

The "I AM" proclamation plays a prominent role in The Law of Attraction teachings and principles. This "I AM", is a declaration to The Universe of having arrived at a place of spiritual maturity. This arrival is marked by an absolute knowing of who and what you are, for if you are one thing, then you cannot be something else.

***

"No matter how hard you squeeze an orange, you will never get apple juice out of it." ~Dr. Wayne Dyer

***

Begin The Day 8 Practice by sitting in meditative contemplation, allow your focus to go as deep in your being as you can imagine. Pose the question inwardly, "Who am I?" Listen intently, as your energy will answer in the most loving of ways. In my personal experience of this process my answer came as: "I am love, I am abundant, I am success, I am compassion, I am handsome, I am smart, I am caring, I am special, and I am uniquely awesome..."

If you would like to reach a place of immovable inner peace, then you must first acknowledge that you are a being of peace. By acknowledging that you are a being of peace, you will have to acknowledge that you have free access to the condition and state of peace. If you have unrestricted access to peace, you can call upon it in an instant and at once be delivered from any external or internal dissonance.

Being peaceful means that you are exerting peace during a certain situation or occasion. To be peace itself means that in all situations, circumstances, and instances you display peace because there is nothing else that you can contribute to life that is not synonymous with peace. In this case, no amount of squeezing (trials, tribulations, or angry drivers) would yield anything un-peaceful from you.

Ironically, and of course, because we all know how great a sense of humor The Universe has, the moment you declare who you are, everything that you are not will start to show up at your doorstep. If you declare in your silent inner temple, with humble assertion, "I AM PEACE", the stage and scene will be set at once that will allow all manner of chaos to enter season 2, episode 1 of the series that is your life. This chaotic nuance my seem at first to be a reprimand by The Universe, but this manifestation of turbulence is a blessing in disguise.

How would The Light know the luminescent brilliance of itself, if not for the darkness? How would you have come to know your fortitude, if not for the challenges of your life? Whether you declare yourself as abundant, loved, cherished, adored, peaceful, happy, joyful, patient, or compassionate, you can be sure that The Universe will eagerly rush in to assist you in rooting yourself in your self-proclaimed "I AM-ness."

Trees gain the ability to stand firm in the face of 50 plus mph winds because they have experienced storms since they were sprouts. As the wind blew harder in a seeming attempt to uproot the little sprout, the future oak tree had to stretch its roots deeper and deeper into the ground. In time, the strength of the oak tree would be the understanding of the sprout: strength lies in rooting oneself.

The Universe wants to help you be peace, so She will give you the perfect people, circumstances, and situations so that you can practice what you are, until you master what you are, then there will only remain the embodiment of what you are = peace.

This is a loving warning of sorts. I found myself bewildered at one point after proclaiming, "I AM ABUNDANT" and "I AM FINANCIALLY FREE." It seemed in the same moment I declared my new found glory, I was blessed with challenge after challenge, after conflict, in opposition to this honor. I first reacted with resistance of course, but my meditation practice became a saving grace; I was able to call upon the stillness I needed. Sitting with my circumstances long enough allowed me to understand the lesson that had presented itself. You see, worry, stress, and anxiety had become a habitual response to money problems in my life. But wait, does a person who is ABUNDANT or who is FINANCIALLY FREE handle financial challenges with worry, fear, or anxiety? "Nope!" I asked myself, "If you were to win the lottery tomorrow, what advice do you think your future self would give you?" My answer, "Chill out!"

Maybe winning the lottery is a long shot, however receiving an unexpected blessing is not. People wake up everyday thinking, "same sh*t different day" and then they surprisingly die. Not to be morbid but it's true. On the opposite end of that spectrum something magical, seemingly unattainable and profound could also be in the cards for you, and you wouldn't even know it or expect it. There are an infinite number of potential future outcomes you could experience revolving around any given situation or circumstance you may find yourself in; so why pick the worst case scenario outcome and hold onto it with reverence?

In order to grasp this concept better, instead of using infinity, I will use the number one billion. If there are one billion possible future outcomes for any given worried, infused situation you find yourself in, what you are saying with your fear/worry/anxiety is that, more than likely out of one billion possible outcomes, "I will surely experience something unsavory." You have a better chance at winning the lottery than you do of experiencing the worst case scenario.

Back to the core message: If The Universe does in fact love me and She knows that I am constantly attempting to evolve and in that evolution, I am beginning to practice using my Divinely inherited creative power, then She will, of course, help me whenever I need assistance. If I am pleading to know myself as the light, God will surely gift me with darkness so that I may shine.

If I am a piece of The Universe, then as I get better, the whole Universe gets better, and if God is for the betterment of all creation, then God is for my personal betterment as well. So, if I decide to root myself in my "I AM ABUNDANT" affirmation, purposefully choosing thoughts saturated with the energetic frequency of abundance, while acting upon any and all opportunities to add financial value to my life, then what we refer to as a "miracle" will surely show up in some profound, unexpected form with Divine timing.

God knows you are trying. If you're reading this, you are giving your attention to this, and if you are giving your attention to this, then you are giving your energy to it. What loving parent wouldn't rejoice at their child giving all their attention to their betterment? Don't you think the parent would even reward the work of the child? The evolution of The Universe is co-creative, you are in a partnership with God. As you continue to evolve through challenges and setbacks, all of creation will be better equipped to deal with challenges and setbacks as a result of your memoir.

If you want to become what you are – in this case, peace – then you must know that no matter what, peace is in fact who you are. For this to happen, you must come face to face with that which is not peace. If you can stand in your place of peace even amid a seeming catastrophe like a tree in the face of a hurricane, you will surely experience yourself as that which you seek. The unpleasant challenges of your life are not meant to be challenges at all. They are meant to be opportunities for practice and growth.

If "ye have faith as a grain of mustard seed, ye shall say unto this mountain, remove hence to yonder place; and it shall remove; and nothing shall be impossible unto you."~Matthew 17:20

Day 9

WHAT DO YOU FEAR?

Peace reflects a conscious one-ness with God. What is there to fear if you are one with The Creator of all things, even if those things seem to be constructed of dismay? Being conscious of your unity with God will negate any free will choice consecrated in uneasiness.

Your conscious unity with The Intelligence may be blocked by the thick fog of your fears; yet no matter where you may find yourself, you will also find God (if you look...). However, what good is this super-power to you if you cannot perceive it? Believing that God is attached to you is a superpower; it produces a level of "allowing" within a person that totally opens them up in such a way that a miracle can be called upon as easy as an inhalation of air. But faith is hard to come by when that distant flickering light (God/faith/hope) is masked by a blanket of thick smoke (your fears), making darkness appear to be the only implied companion.

When you make choices allowing your fears to captain your vessel, you will tend to sail away from that which you desire. Instead, you will likely head exactly into the perfect storm you are trying to avoid. Our fears and how they guide us may work in surprising ways. It may appear to us that we are making choices to protect our well-being, when in fact we are the baby bird in the nest who has just gotten so comfortable that we have forgotten we have wings. We cannot avoid the fact that, the path to our highest possible good will undoubtedly lead us through The Dark Forest of our most deeply imbued trepidations.

There is an Ogre that guards the bridge which you must pass over in order to get to The Magical Castle of Your Dreams. In the face of your monsters what will you do? Will you walk forward, believing The Most High is standing right beside you, or will you, in your perceived solitude, settle here, for "good enough"?

On the bright side of things, fear can be a gift if it is allowed to be such. It is the resistance (fear) and the pushing through this resistance by you that builds the muscles of spiritual masters. Godly confidence is the side effect of overcoming one's fears. What do you imagine can be accomplished with such Holy brashness?

***

So now, "What do you fear?"
***

For the Day 9 Practice I would like for you to write a sincere list of all your fears. Going down your list one at a time, again with honest sincerity, ask yourself, "Why do I fear______?" Be careful as to make sure you pull this weed up by the root. A true, deep-seated fear will be masked by multiple levels of other fears. In searching for this truth, imagine that your true fears are at the sub-atomic level; constantly push yourself to look deeper. You will instinctively know when you have reached the absolute core of a fear.

For example, you may list "fear of failure" as one of your fears. When asking yourself, "Why do I fear failure?", you may respond with something like, "I don't want people to look down on me." A more thorough search would yield a response something like, "I don't want people to look down on me because it makes me feel like I'm not good enough." Searching even deeper reveals, "My biological father wasn't in my life and he never even sought out a relationship with me." Deeper we go, "Because my own father didn't even want to be in my life, I believe at my core, I am truly unworthy of anyone's love, because I wasn't even worthy of my own father's love." It may now perhaps be somewhat easier to see how something like, "fear of failure" is really about a sense of worth which relates to a sense of well-being. So someone may (on the surface) fear failure, but really what they fear is that their sense of well being will be compromised if they fail.

Deeply searching through your fears can be a very beneficial tool for a few reasons. First, when you get to the root cause of your fears, you will be able to shed light on and thus heal the fear, transforming a curse into a blessing. The healing experienced as a result of the work you have done, will allow you to live your life lighter, more peacefully, and from a place of acceptance and faith. Second, you will begin to notice that many surface level frustrations and irritations are actually the result of a deeper fear.

Pausing to search for the true origin of the surface level irritation will enable you to come to situations which previously may have caused chaos, with a loving curiosity. You may ask yourself, "Why is this person's driving (which I have no control over) upsetting me so much?" Personally, my surface level irritations and frustrations are usually a result of being hungry or not getting enough sleep the night before. Even now, I still have to pause amid my irritations and ask myself, "why?" The line of questioning and refusal to accept anything less than a core cause will allow me to arrive at the question, "Have you eaten yet today?" So, sometimes, you may be more irritable because of something other than a fear. The lesson here is to pause and seek.

***

"Why is this really bothering me?"
***

You can use this question every time you are irritated by someone or something. Never cease to go within, every answer to every question can be found there. Either external things will constantly annoy you, or you will negate those nuances by searching for the deeper meaning and opportunity for healing that they present. The latter perspective will dramatically change your life for the better.

Day 10

BECOMING SELF SERVING

Do you think it's your responsibility to save the world? You probably do have some responsibility to assist with the transformation of Gaia; however, your first responsibility will be to yourself and your overall mental, physical, emotional, and spiritual health and well-being.

Let's say that each day you're given a pitcher of water from Uni. This water is 100% all-natural, organic, non-gmo God essence, with the ability to heal, transform, enlighten, create miracles, and much more. You have the ability to pour this water into any vessel you choose each day and because you feel a responsibility to **your** world, your daily supply of water is used to fill your partner's vessel, your children's vessel, the vessel of your career, your parent's vessel, and the vessels of your family and friends. After the day has concluded, you feel productive as you consider yourself a savior of sorts for tending to the needs of those you love.

But wait one minute! By the time you have finished filling everyone else's vessel, you have no more water to fill your own vessel. Over time and as you continue to constantly serve the well-being of others, you come to grasp that resentfulness is the only thing you are filled with.

Expecting others to give as freely and openly to you as you do to them, is a total misconception, stemming from the misunderstanding of an unspoken agreement between you and the people in your life. The stance of, "give...give...give" while receiving nothing in return results in feelings of antipathy, animosity, and aversion, which are not synonymous with peace.

Instead of attempting to fulfill others' needs, the Day 10 Practice asks you to first fulfill your own needs, whether that means taking some time away from the husband and kids, or saying, "No" today where you constantly said "Yes" yesterday.

Referring to the water-pitcher analogy, imagine what would happen if you left your water-pitcher under The Universe's tap each day and never moved it. What would begin to happen after the first day of total fulfillment is that your cup will "runneth over", and that is the point! If you were to continually make sure that your vessel is always filled with this 100% All-Natural God Essence from The Garden of Eden Mountain Springs, what will eventually happen is that this water would overflow onto the floor, then into all the rooms of your house, followed by flowing into the streets, until your whole neighborhood is flooded with The Universe's love.

If you become so fulfilled with God that only God flows from you as a natural result of a brimming cup that more water is added to, you will be assisting in changing the world to a more beautiful, brighter, and more accepting place simply by your presence.

This worldly transformation can be accomplished by making sure all your needs—spiritual, emotional, and physical—are met before you try to assist others with their needs. If you need more rest, make sure you get it. If you need more free time, make sure you request it. If you need to feel more love, pamper yourself. Take a nap, go for a drive alone, treat yourself to some ice cream for doing such a good job at being you! You need love too! So, remember to give yourself all the love you can, so that you can give the world the best part of you!

Day 11

A THEORY IN SUBCONSCIOUS CONDITIONING

You're in an argument with your significant other and both of your voices keep increasing in octaves as you try to force your understanding upon the other, because maybe they just can't hear you well enough to comprehend your perspective.

You end up "winning" the argument as your partner is essentially forced to accept your point of view in hopes of a peace treaty being signed. This "win" at once creates a positive correlation in the subconscious mind between the use of force and success. The subconscious mind will now hold this relationship between coercive behavior and reward as a sure means to acquire success whenever it draws up any plans of action regarding the attainment or realization of an ideal. What this now means is that, every time you want something, you may believe that if nothing else, the use of force will yield it to you. All you must do is pray louder and harder and you can have anything you want.

How would you really like to obtain success? How does obtaining success through a gentle understanding and allowing sound? Pertaining to misunderstandings in relationships, if one person wins, the other person must lose. If you are participating in this 30-Day practice, then I will assume that always having to beat someone to nirvana is not how you would like to live your life.

Peace would constitute an understanding amid a disagreement resulting in a healing. Understanding is never reached through force. Understanding is the result of comprehension. Comprehension is reached through a willingness to search out the truth. Willingness is the key component of the journey to discernment. Willingness corresponds to allowing. Allowing is at the opposite end of the spectrum from coercion. In the case of arguing with a partner, what could you do to try and understand where the other person is coming from while gently allowing them to see your perspective? You could find success through a willingness to understand.

Can you come to every misunderstanding between yourself and another with a willingness to understand? If you can seek a more gentle perspective, you can find a new dimension of realization which would hand over a heavenly reward: understanding. Do we not all seek to be understood on a deeper level? For the world to know us beyond our flaws and tribulations? If this is the case, then why not give that which you seek to everyone you encounter? Now if you accomplish this constant understanding, then you can become the energy of understanding, and if you are understanding itself, then how can the world misunderstand you?

The Day 11 Practice asks that you try and apply understanding to your next disagreement with another. See if you can, through attentiveness, find out empathetically, why the other person feels the way they do. Put yourself in their shoes and come to the disagreement attempting to see things from their perspective. Using a statement like, "I can see why you feel this way..." can disarm the other person. What they really hear you saying is, "your perspective and your feelings are valued..." If conflicts arise due to misunderstanding, then comprehension will equate to accord. This methodology towards understanding will hinge on you making a genuine effort to see the other person's point of view, even if you feel they are absolutely wrong. Most people just want to be heard and their feelings to be validated.

Note: It is essential to your well-being that you make the distinction between being loving and being mistreated and disrespected. Never allow someone else to take advantage of your love. If you continually come from a place of understanding in your dealings with someone while they continually come from a place of anger/fear, then I would advise you re-evaluate the relationship. The goal is to give understanding so that the other person will feel safe enough to give the same thing to you. When you are in a relationship where understanding is the goal of both parties then your relationship will reflect love and peace at its highest degree.

Day 12

"THIS IS MY SHOW!"

Life has taken me to some pretty awesome places with a wide variety of flavorful experiences. I have had the pleasure of working in a very awesome and beautifully out-of-place coffee shop in the coastal South. I nicknamed the shop, "the trendy misfit". It was at this place that one of my most useful affirmations was born, "THIS IS MY SHOW!"

As order after order piled in, customers began to grow increasingly eager, as if waiting for the last rations of food in a post-apocalyptic movie scene. I, of course, was trying my very best to deliver each order with swiftness and accuracy, but at once it seemed as if I was beginning to be slowly taken under as if making skinny cappuccinos in quicksand. Right before I took my last breath of air, in comes my wonderfully Divine friend, Intuition.

In the midst of the chaos a calm reassuring thought came to the surface of my consciousness, "THIS IS YOUR SHOW!" ...I paused for a moment and replied with a "DAMN RIGHT!" In that moment I realized that my best was all I had to offer and that was enough. An extremely calming energy flowed over my entire body like a cool breeze on a hot summer day as I fell into flow with The Universe. Before, I had been fighting against the current of busyness; after I received a love note from my Intuition, I let go. I allowed the busyness to be there with my gentle acceptance. Ironically, my instance of acceptance shifted the energy of the entire coffee shop. A calm came over each and every customer as a result of the inner peace I was able to display. It was like magic. Time seemingly slowed down as latte after latte was handed over to patiently grateful hands.

It seems in this human experience that we aim for Godly perfection sometimes, to make sure deadlines, desires, needs, wants, and plans are executed with flawless efficiency and accuracy. However, we may fall short in our attempts at perfection, only accomplishing the feeling of disappointment entwined with the energy of "overdoing" it.

My affirmation meant that, this and any other situation I found myself to be in literally belonged to me, intimately orchestrated in a co-creative partnership between The Universe and myself. This also meant that in this particular coffee shop example, the stage had been set for me to truly experience exactly who I was. How does the light truly know its capability for brightness, if not for the dark? How do the strong come to know their true power, if not for a challenge? How can there be courage, if there is nothing that brings up fear? In that moment I understood that this was an opportunity for me to be peace itself, rooting myself in heavenly tranquility.

Having the belief that God and I teamed up to bring this particular experience and opportunity to me gave me a surreal level of confidence. If this was in fact my creation, then I knew there would be nothing in it that could truly harm me. Peace is the result of a deep understanding that nothing can truly be taken away from you because The Universe is all-inclusive. If God is omnipresent, God is always nearby. If The Universe is all-inclusive who/what exists that can truly take something away? If there is only this vast ocean, who could steal a cup of water from it? If God is for me, then what could possibly be against me?

The Day 12 Practice asks that you use the affirmation "This is my show!" in your life whenever things are seemingly getting out of control. If you can make the act of pausing a habitual course of action in regards to the ever-changing demands of life, then you will surely reach a state of immovable inner peace. This affirmation places the power back in your hands as you begin to demonstrate your co-creative partnership with The Universe.

Day 13

FINDING THE FLOW

When you find yourself in the middle of your next challenging experience, ask yourself, "What is the path of least resistance?"

Gentle and harmonic, the energy of God is at constant flow. Resembling the tender, rhythmic cadence of a heartbeat or the subtly shifting ocean currents, The Universe is all about melodic concordance. Just think of The Universe as one big song, constantly being played, always changing and evolving. Since we are all together in this choir, we need to all harmonize as well.

Being right vs. being happy is at the heart of finding the flow. What is it that you think you need to be, do, or say versus what is the most gentle approach in a given moment of discord? Let's say that you must deal with the medical industry due to being a caretaker of someone you love, or because you have a health challenge yourself. File this, call this number, go here, ask for Ms. Sanders, make sure you get form 45T...the list goes on. Frustrated due to witnessing the perceived lack of compassion displayed by the medical industry, you become upset because it feels like you're alone and it feels like the people who should be helping you are actually setting you back or delaying you. How could you find peace in this situation or any other situations like this?

I used to play a game with Uni. When things would start to seem as if it were Me vs. The World, I would immediately start to let go, and accept the challenge. I accepted the rudeness and apparent lack of humanity in those I was dealing with. Feeling like I was being unfairly treated, I would pause in an attempt to determine what was really at the base of all my irritations. Examination revealed that, of course it usually came back to me and my fears.

A while back I found myself in a battle with my local DMV as well as the DMV from another state. I intrinsically knew that I was "right." It didn't help my case that every time I explained the circumstances and situations to anyone else, they all agreed it was a bunch of (insert expletive). At one point I found myself on the phone genuinely questioning the "are you serious-ness" of the person on the other line. It was like trying to convince someone blind and deaf that it wasn't raining outside, when they were convinced that it was.

So, what did I do? I practiced radical acceptance. If God is for me, who can be against me? If Uni is co-creating my reality every second with me, then even this (insert expletive) must be The Universe, too. So, if Uni is here, She must be trying to show/teach me something. I thought to myself, *Why don't you just let go and see where you end up.* So, I let go.

My experiences with Uni earlier on in my life resulted with Her needing to "force" my blessings upon me. What I mean by that is that God always has a much larger and more encompassing perspective than we currently have, and therefore He can see and understand things which we aren't even aware exist. This being the case and due to God's love for us, She knows the best way that will lead us (each individually) back home to one-ness/heaven/nirvana. But to be honest, I wasn't really trying to learn all the lessons, gain more wisdom and knowledge, do the work, and heal. What I was really trying to do was, win the Powerball Jackpot, go to Six Flags, and go on a vacation with all my favorite people; I just wanted to play and have fun. I still want those things but in order to embody the highest version of myself, I needed to have trials and tribulations. In order to know that God and I were one, I had to journey to that place of knowing.

As you are able to witness the totality of the entire journey, you will come to know your ultimate truth the moment you arrive at the destination you seek. If you seek peace, you will certainly experience its antonym, however when you reach a place of immovable peace, you will be able to see how every mistake, misstep, or misfortune was just a simple steppingstone to your objective. Your ultimate truth is that you are okay, and you will always be at the very least okay.

Resistance is not how God works. Resistance in the spiritual realm implies a need to use force to obtain that which is already yours through your Divine Inheritance. Using force to obtain what you already have is an insane act. In my DMV example I came to understand and accept how going with the flow was a power tool.

Fast forward to the present moment: I can feel the very subtle changes in the wind and adjust my sails accordingly. I have let go of the idea that I know exactly what the best route for me to sail is. Previously in my experience, I would hold onto this idea of what I thought was best for me. Attempting to bring this manifestation of my perceived best life to the tangible, time and time again I was met with resistance from people, places, things, situations, and experiences. I finally gave up, and not being salty at all about it, I gave control of the helm to Uni.

***

"Jesus take the wheel!"

***

Handing over control of your life and destiny to God is undoubtedly scary. Personally, I was afraid mainly because I didn't know if God's plans for me were as fun as my plans for myself, plus adding in the fear of constantly being in the unknown was scary for me. I had no idea what "blessings" masked as problems awaited me with Uni as the captain of my ship. I did, however, understand that with or without God leading my life, there was still the factor of the unknown that I had to accept. Acceptance of the unknown meant that I had to come to a realization; either Uni existed and wanted the best for me or there was no such thing as Uni.

My ability to "trust the process" and "go with the flow" came as a result of remembering all the instances when something amazing happened to me in my favor that was totally out of my control. *Okay, I thought... I know Uni loves me, I also know that I can't see exactly where I am going, and I don't know what other things are traveling at light speed towards me right now that are meant to assist me, but I know that if God is really real, then I have to bet the house on Her every time.* So, I did. I still feel the emotions of fear, doubt, frustration, and impatience growing ever so slightly within me, attempting to sprout through to the surface. However, I feel the feelings while allowing them to pass through me; that is the key.

For the Day 13 Practice, I ask you to constantly seek the path of least resistance while weighing the option of being right versus being happy. A power tool in this practice would be to constantly remind yourself that The Universe has your back by recounting every instance you received a timely blessing in your life. Keeping a "miracle journal" is a great exercise to assist you in your development. Basically, each day you would recount a blessing (big or small) and write it in your journal. Over the course of a year, you will have a journal that is filled with reminders of God's love and with this you will gain confidence to let go when it is time to do so.

If you seek out a compromise that is for the highest good of all involved when dealing with your next challenge, then you will be consciously seeking peace. If you are using a magnifying glass to find dirt, you will find dirt even in the cleanest of places. The same analogy holds true in regards to constantly searching for peace; even in the most chaotic of situations, you will be able to find even the smallest traces of tranquil harmonies.

A note from me:

Always fight for what you love. Always fight for justice. There may be times in your life where you are met with staunch resistance in regards to a goal. This goal may pertain to a deeper injustice that you are experiencing or witnessing. Sometimes doing the right thing in this case may be the most challenging. It is during these times that you have to listen intently to your heart; some battles are worth fighting. It is only when good men do nothing, that evil prevails.

Day 14

FINDING YOUR
EQUILIBRIUM

In between challenge and harmony, in the middle of success and defeat, in the midst of deadline and schedule, who are you?

Who are you when things are manageable?

Who are you when there are bills to be paid, but you feel confident in your ability to meet the terms?

Where is your middle point?

Finding your equilibrium point can be quite useful on the path to inner peace because it is from this place of equilibrium that you will want to respond when posed with challenging people, places, situations and experiences.

If someone is offering you anger or negativity, would you like to respond from a place where you are out of balance and angry yourself or, would you like to respond from a place of balance, where your emotions are in check, and your responses are rooted in the rational mind? One of these ripostes will assist you in reaching the summit of your 30-Day journey, while the other will assure that you remain at base camp. If you can feel anger within your being but you are still able to pause before reacting while asking yourself, "Am I reacting from a place of who I truly am or am I reacting from a place of out of balance-ness", then you will radically begin to transform your life.

You will not be able to control how other people treat you, or the way in which the external world engages you, but you will be able to control how you respond to those uncertain demands. The people that we interact with the most can give us the perfect environment to practice peace. In many romantic relationships, due to the constant interactions and sharing of the same environment, there will naturally be disagreements. These disagreements may often be accompanied with high emotions, the scale sliding between love and acceptance to frustration, annoyance, anger, and/or irritation.

When we feel passionate about something, the feeling associated with that passion seems to be all encompassing, filling our entire being. If you add that in many relationships, we let things build up over time because we fail to properly communicate our wants and needs, then when the right buttons are pushed, the pot boils over and someone gets burned; throwing hot water on someone you love isn't such a nice thing to do. In order to overcome the cycle of mere reactions in this case, the act of pausing to determine where exactly you will be responding from is key.

If you consider yourself to be a happy, peaceful, compassionate, and helpful person most of the time, then those adjectives may qualify as your point of equilibrium. Now if you struggle with being happy, peaceful, compassionate, and helpful, that's perfectly fine, too. If you're one of those individuals, your equilibrium point will be defined as the emotional/mental state where you feel the most naturally at peace and calm.

When external circumstances are peaceful and serene, it is easy to embody saintliness. However, when things are tumultuous, responding peacefully is a lot more challenging. Luckily, these challenging situations will set the stage for enlightening work. Due to the challenge of attempting to respond to negativity with positivity, you will begin to exercise what I have deemed as your "Peace Muscle." The more you hit the gym, i.e., are involved in challenging situations, and you work out your Peace Muscle, the stronger that muscle becomes.

In order to work out the Peace Muscle, you must always make an attempt to come from your place of equilibrium, no matter what is being offered to you in exchange. Fun stuff, I know. If you use the Peace Muscle and gym analogy whenever you find yourself face to face with seeming unfairness and anger, you can add a bit of lightheartedness and humor to the situation. You can say to yourself, "Okay, I could curse him/her out, or I could just hit the gym with this situation, work out my Peace Muscle and get a little more buff! Beach season is approaching anyway. Sun's out, guns out!"

Adding humor to the heaviness of negative, emotionally charged situations, immediately begins to add healing light to the darkness. If you can always pose the question, "Where I am reacting from? A place of peace or a place of frustration?" when dealing with disharmony, then you will consciously begin to reclaim your power. When we react, we are at the will of our emotions, and when was the last time you reacted with anger and achieved salvation?

The Day 14 Practice asks that you find your equilibrium point and constantly attempt to respond from that place, because your equilibrium point is who you truly are; **know yourself**. If you react from a place of love, love will undoubtedly find its way back to you. If you react from a place of anger, anger will undoubtedly find its way back to you. A state of inner peace is more easily obtained when love is constantly given and thus constantly received. This is accomplished by constantly giving your Divine truth, which is love, to everything and everyone you encounter.

Day 15

GOING TO TEMPLE

On your journey to inner peace, a key component of your success will rely on finding your temple and returning to it as much as possible.

Your temple is the place that naturally brings you the most peace, tranquility, and happiness. I have found my temple both in meditation and in nature. When I am immersed in nature, I always find myself engulfed in natural peace and harmony. I can feel the gentle stillness of "happening" vibrating all around me. Even though there may be a lot going on in my life, nature still whispers to me with a Knowing calmness.

Meditation is one of my favorite places to go as well because it is in this place that I can consciously connect my energy with the energy of The Universe, dissolving into at-one-ment with Source. Neither nature nor my meditative practice ever asks anything of me, yet everything is given to me. In nature and in my mediation practice alike, a great deal of silence fills the space, even while so many intricate processes are taking place. God's genius work appears effortless; simple being-ness equates to grandeur.

The more time I spend in my temple, the more I am reminded of my ultimate truth; *I am a unique part of both nature and God; therefore I can be at peace because I am aware of my eternal oneness with All That Is.* The day-to-day activities in my experience of being human make it easy for me to forget the magic that I am a part of: the wants, needs, desires, fears, doubts, and frustrations I experience daily. If nature and my body can succeed in carrying out an almost infinite number of complex processes each minute with seeming gentleness and ease, then what can I *not* accomplish? Am I not the same as what I am a part of?

Your temple can be wherever you want it to be. Perhaps you feel supremely connected with The Most High when you write. Maybe you feel one with God when you sing. Gardening or yoga may make you feel the closest to All That Is. Your temple will be unique to you. The more you go to your temple, the more peace you will find in both your internal and external worlds.

The Day 15 Practice asks that you find your temple (the place where you feel closest to Spirit) and try to return to that place as much as you possibly can.

Day 16

THE MINI MIRACLE LIST

On my personal journey to inner peace, I kept a journal specifically to write down all my daily interactions with Uni. I entitled my findings, "The Mini Miracle List."

Each day I recorded something that I considered to be a mini miracle or interaction with The Universe. I jotted down the big and the small, whether that was riding the bus for free, being treated to lunch, or affirming that I was a "money-magnet" then finding a penny on the ground. Looking for how God worked in my life became a habitual game. I found myself constantly on the lookout for even the smallest of miracles. My Mini Miracle List game was fun, and the more I looked for mini-miracles and God, the more I found them both.

An intent search for God will result in finding Her. My Mini Miracle List implied that I was seeking out a personal relationship with Jehovah by asking from a soul place, "How do you work in my life?" The Universe gets very excited whenever we begin to seek a relationship and partnership with Her. One of the goals of this human experience is to come to truly understand and know ourselves as God. The illusion of separation is created to give us a plane of reality to discover this truth. Simply being told that we are God may correlate to doubt and uncertainty regarding our true nature; we may even feel blasphemous. At times we may seem to be engulfed in darkness, but only so that we may experience our truth—that *we* are the light.

This experience on Earth can be very challenging at times because we must negate what we see and hear and follow a feeling/the intangible in order to successfully reach our ultimate destination we set out to accomplish through our incarnation here. If you can constantly disregard what your senses are revealing, while relying on an innate feeling that you are in fact "going the right way", you will eventually reach that heaven on earth, accomplishing one of the goals that you set out to accomplish when your soul materialized on this plane.

You are, and always will be, connected with God in your heart. This connection will tell you if something is right or wrong for you. Sometimes opportunities may appear to be perfect on the surface, but your internal GPS brings up feelings of apprehension. The opposite is true as well, sometimes opportunities may appear to be daunting on the surface while your internal GPS is telling you that you are in fact, "going the right way."

By creating your own, "Mini Miracle List," you will consequently begin to seek out The Universe's friendship, enabling you to see all the instances of Great Spirit's presence in your life. Perhaps the most important benefit of this list is that you will be notating all the breadcrumbs you encounter on your way back home. As the journey home is faith-based, sometimes you may seem to be lost or you may feel that things are not working out for you, but if you are constantly taking note of the small gestures from The Universe, then life's unknown doesn't feel so discouraging.

For the Day 16 Practice, start a Mini Miracle List of your own. Write down all the signs you see from Spirit each day, starting today. Dictate each magical happenstance, no matter how big or small. Take note of each bread crumb God left you on your path to remind you, *Everything is going to be okay.* At the end of each week, go over your list while remembering your feelings regarding each entry.

Day 17

REMEMBER...LET GO

Let go of the need to be right.
Let go the need to have things turn out exactly as planned.
Let go of fear.
Let go of struggle.
Let go of the idea of perfection.
Let go of guilt.
Let go of the idea of how success looks.
Let go of anger.
Let go of resentment.
Let go of blame.

Your co-creative partnership with The Universe will become more evident to you as time goes on. In such, you will receive Divine guidance, motivation, and inspiration at the exact right time. Patience is synonymous with peace as faith is undertaken as a rebuttal for uneasy eagerness. The faith corresponds to an energetic reverberance of trust that God always has your best interest in mind. If you can faithfully accept that The Universe is constantly working behind the scenes on your behalf, then tranquility will become an easily reachable stance in almost every occasion.

When I was initially writing this Day 18 Practice, I started with a totally different title and message. As I sat down at my computer to write, my thoughts seemed a bit more congested than usual. Though I was able to write a few paragraphs, upon re-reading what I had written, I felt that my words lacked the magic of the previous chapters. I must admit that I am little more tired than usual right now, but I decided to write anyway because I gave myself a deadline. In my mind, I *had* to write today, and I also *had* to stay on track with my deadline. At once remembering in a Holy instant how Uni works in my life, while recalling the co-creative nature of this work and all other work I do, I decided to walk away from the computer and take a nap.

When The Universe and I are in unison, I feel it and know it without a doubt; sometimes it's almost as if I go into a blackout, typing away furiously without effort. Tonight, I felt as if I lacked my magical partner, and I knew it. So, when walking away from the computer, I gently reminded myself, "Remember...let go." In the very next moment..."whoosh!!!", in came a flurry of Divinely creative inspiration. This whole occurrence was such a wonderful learning experience for me because I got to witness *again* that The Universe always has my highest good in mind.

For me, "letting go" meant getting rid of the idea that I had to finish this *30 Day Guide To Inner Peace* by a certain date. I do have other projects that will need my attention soon, and I am excited about giving this guidebook to the world, but no one is going to die if I don't have it finished by a certain date. I pray this work will add relief to as many people's souls as possible. Perhaps someone may need to have a certain experience in his or her life that hasn't yet transpired in order to fully understand some of the truths present within these pages. I am a part of something much bigger than myself; therefore, I must remember that it's not just about me and my needs. *The 30-Day Guide To Inner*

Peace will be done in Divine perfect timing, because it is for the highest good of all involved.

When we can look at our lives and our actions from a higher perspective, visualizing the multitude of puzzle pieces independently embarking on a journey to completeness, unknowingly seeking a vast togetherness, it is easier to understand that harmony dictates the fact that dissimilar notes find congruence among themselves. As an independent puzzle piece and musical note yourself, you will find an ease in discovering this congruence the moment you let go of your need to hold onto your perhaps narrow perspective of things. You will experience more harmony in your life as a result of facilitating flow through acts of letting go (allowing). The consequence of holding on to something is that you will have to constrict. How can Heavenly Love flow to and through you if you are constricted?

Getting lost in wanting things to happen exactly as planned can be quite easy, but of what advantage to your soul is that? What if everything always happened just how, when, and where you wanted? Nothing would ever be better than expected. There would be no surprises. There would be no synchronistic events. More importantly, God wouldn't have a place to start a relationship with you.

One of the coolest things I am finding out about life is that we each have a unique way in which God works with us to bring our highest ideal to the world of form; I think that is very special! For me it means God and I are bringing to life an idea *we* share, which is even more amazing! Reminding myself of this partnership can be challenging at times because I can get transfixed on having things happens just as I have envisioned. The fear lies in me thinking that if I let go of my vision, things won't be as good as they could have been, and I'll be the only one to blame for my shortcomings. However, if I can constantly remind myself that God is my partner in all of this, then I can at least have faith that even though things may look different or evolve differently than

I had envisioned, everything will still turn out surprisingly wonderful! So far Uni has not let me down whenever I have decided to hand over my plans of grandiosity to The Holiest of editors.

The Day 17 Practices asks that, whether you're running late for work or you feel like your next vacation needs to be planned with perfect execution so that everyone will have the most fun possible, try letting go some. See what happens when you give Spirit room to work in your life. Maybe you're running late so that you can see or hear something you wouldn't have if you had been on time. If you're supposed to meet someone, or have a conversation, or be at a certain place at a certain time, all for your highest good and for the advancement of your soul, know that, without a doubt, God will rearrange heaven and earth on your behalf to ensure that things line up for you.

Day 18

WHAT NO LONGER
SERVES YOU?

Do you feel as if gossiping would serve your highest good if you were attempting to reach a place of immovable inner peace?

Do you think being judgmental would serve your highest good if you were attempting to reach a place of immovable inner peace?

What about being impatient?

How about dwelling on the past?

What do you think about unbridled anger?

Do you think holding on to resentment will equate to peace?

You have been with *You* your whole life, which means that in this exact moment, *You* know exactly what no longer serves your highest good on your quest to inner peace. Whatever those things may be, gently begin to release them.

In the experience of being human we will continue to relive some of the same dissatisfactory experiences of old, in a new place, and with new people because we have missed the opportunity to give something different to a reoccurring circumstance. We may find ourselves to be chronic saboteurs, constantly spreading fear where we could have been spreading love. Albert Einstein put it quite perfectly, "The definition of insanity is doing the same thing over and over again yet expecting different results." What have you been doing that has continually led you down the same path time and time again? Maybe it's time to turn left where you normally would have turned right.

Relationships are a wonderful platform for you to discover and begin to heal the issues which may have been holding you back until now. In the past, I believed that I was broken at my core due to the absence of my biological father in my life. This belief laid the foundation for me to be happily dishonest and to push people away in my most intimate relationships. I placed the blame on others anytime things were in disarray.

Living from a place of fear, lashing out with anger as a result of that fear, all the while being manipulative, caused me to squander away some of the most magical soulmate relationships that I have had the pleasure of experiencing. However, a bit of time had to pass before I identified some of my most detrimental habits and it took even longer to heal the fears at the foundation of those habits. Honestly, multiple lifetimes could have passed before I was able to let go of what no longer served me. The Universe had my back, though, and Uni always wants the absolute best for me, so when I made the conscious decision to live life from my highest possible ideal, I was shown everything that I needed to let go of in order to spread my wings and fly.

Letting go in general will be one of easiest as well as most challenging things you will be asked to do on your journey to inner peace. Fear is the main cause. A secondary challenge will be changing your mind about something in order to break an old habit. Habits are so easily formed in the human mind, and as a result, anger may simply be the most natural response you have to fear, frustration, irritation, or another's anger. Judgment may be another natural response to a deepseated, unhealed fear. A tool you can use in this practice is to begin to notice what your natural responses are in different situations which cause you any internal annoyance. If you can pinpoint the moment and cause of any of your habitual responses of anger or fear, you can also in that same instance ask yourself, "Why did I respond in that manner?" If you can pause, even amid rising emotions, you will begin to take back control of your life and your destiny.

Breaking the habitual responses you have developed over the course of your life will seem daunting at first but, The Grand Canyon wonderfully illustrates what can happen with gentle persistence. If gently flowing water can cut through rock, imagine what you can accomplish with consistent, gently flowing love and peace. Be attentive to your responses amid any extreme emotions or situations which would typically cause you to react. Instead, try to find your equilibrium before you respond.

The Day 18 Practice asks that you let go of your habitual responses. Tell the truth when you are tempted to be dishonest. Show restraint where you normally would have displayed lack of discipline. Seek patience in situations that agitate you. Use positive affirmations as a rebuttal to thoughts rooted in fear and anxiety. Solicit understanding instead of judgment. Begin to tell a new story, one filled with love, with patience, with kindness, with compassion, and with peace; you are becoming a butterfly, after all. If a situation or thought cannot assist you in reaching a state of sublime inner peace, avoid it or discard it. A multitude of blessings are waiting to fill the void left behind by letting go of that which no longer serves you.

Day 19

PEACE THROUGH FORGIVENESS

It is now time to forgive it all.

Forgive the past.

Forgive others who have hurt you.

Forgive the world for being unfair.

Above all else, forgive yourself, it is time...

You've finally got the ticket and now you're about to embark on your journey to your dream destination. You've waited your entire life for this moment, so much so that when the day of your departure arrives, it feels surreal.

You arrive at the airport to check in. Everything is going smoothly until you get to the luggage check. The attendant tells you that your suitcase is overweight, and you cannot board the plane until your suitcase is under the maximum allowable weight requirement. You feel flustered and apprehensive as you come to the realization that you literally must throw away some of your stuff in order to go on your trip.

You've been packing your whole life for this trip and every meaningful situation, experience, person, place, or thing that has ever happened to you is in this suitcase. Some of the things you've packed hold such sentimental value that you feel like they're an extension of who you are. You ask yourself, "How am I going to choose which things I have to leave behind when I've held on to so many of them for so long??"

In order to board the plane and fly to your dream destination of peace, happiness, or heavenly nirvana, you must lighten your load. Two of the items that we may all have in common in our suitcases are blame and condemnation. Life can be challenging.

Throughout the course of your experience of being human, you have undoubtedly done things to hurt others, and others have done things to hurt you. Some of these experiences may have had such a profound impact on you that they seem to be interwoven into your being, becoming an extension of who you are.

The negative experiences we endure tend to root themselves at the core of our being, convoluting and interlacing within the fabric of our happiness. Fear and apprehension develop as a natural response to any opportunity to experience joy and love because we have weeds of hurt and pain imbedded in our rose garden. The beauty is hard to see and accept because we have held onto the tribulations of the past, remembering them, therefore nurturing them, therefore facilitating their growth. As we are beings of light, made of pure energy, whatever we give our attention to, we also give our light and love to, and where there is love, you will find growth.

If you would like your life to reflect the absolute best, full of love, joy, and peace, then you will have to lighten your load. You will have to pull the weeds of pain and suffering that are in your rose garden. In order to board the plane that will take you to your dreams, you will have to remove all the articles in your internal suitcase that do not reverberate love, because love reverberates forgiveness, and forgiveness reverberates healing.

What are you holding onto from your past? Who hurt you? What deeds done in secret have you propagated, only to be left with guilt as an after effect? Whatever it may be, whoever it may have been, or whatever you may have done, forgive it all. Give it all up. Let it go. Of course, this is easier said than done, and you probably won't be able to forgive your entire past overnight. It took me years of internal work to forgive others and to forgive myself. In this regard I am still currently on the path of healing and forgiveness. Forgiveness is challenging yet fulfilling work. Your journey of inner healing and forgiveness, however, will unquestionably reveal the inner God/Goddess that lies dormant within your spirit.

The human body does a wonderful job of releasing wastes and toxins through sweat and even tears, amongst a multitude of other means, some a little too gross to discuss here. Due to the amount of pain and discomfort some memories or events may cause us, ignoring them can seem far easier than facing them. Because of this avoidance and denial, emotional toxins can become imbedded in our bodies, which when ignored can manifest into physical illness or disease. So, if you haven't done so already, make crying a conscious practice. If you feel frustrated, annoyed, or irritated, it is perfectly fine to excuse yourself and go release that energy with a good cry. Remember, The Universe is all about flow, and crying is an act of liberation. Liberation equates to freedom, freedom equates to allowing, allowing is synonymous with God.

Crying is a sign that you are releasing the pain, the guilt, the anger, and the shame of the past. Crying is a sign that a healing is taking place.

On my journey to inner healing, I cried more than I have ever cried in my entire life. I cried from the hurt I felt, I cried when I forgave others, I cried when I forgave myself, I even cried during nostalgic movie scenes. I felt as if I needed a good cry at least once per week. I cried so much because I had so much pent-up emotional energy that I had been holding onto for years, simply because "men don't cry." As I cried, I began to let go, and as I let go, I began to heal. As I healed, I felt lighter. The lighter I felt, the happier I felt. The happier I felt, the more at peace I felt.

With the body, as with the soul, issues will come to the surface in hopes of being healed! Watch out for full moons! At first there will be a gentle nudge to address a certain discordance within your soul, but when these tender prods are continually ignored, a much more startling method will be needed to grab your attention. From experience, I know catching God on the whisper is 100 times better than being forced to act later. You will heal your soul either in this lifetime or another, but you will constantly be given the opportunity to come home. Good old fear will be an ever present companion on the road to healing but the age-old spiritual motto, "Feel the fear and do it anyway" is especially true in this case. If you choose to avoid those deeply entrenched, hindering nuances of emotional bereavement that have come to the forefront of your being in order to be healed, the challenges and discomfort you will face will be severe at best.

Who is it that you need to forgive in this moment? The first person that pops in your mind is the person who needs your unfettering. I know some of you may have experienced the seemingly unpardonable, however the forgiveness is not for them, it is to liberate you. It is true that you can move mountains with a small amount of faith. In order to forgive the most deplorable, you must employ an act of faith and belief that everything that has and that will happen to you is in the hands of a Loving Creator. With this faith, you could never be a victim; instead, you will constantly search each misfortune you experience for the opportunity to become a master of your reality. You will come to understand that everything you experience is **your** creation. My question to you is this: "Can you begin to look for the good in the seeming bad?"

If you do not forgive your past, you will unfortunately be unable to move forward on your spiritual path and live your highest ideal. If you cannot allow forgiveness to fill your vessel, you will not be able to board the plane that will take you to your dreams. Wonderful things will certainly happen to you regardless, however; Uni's cool like that! But over time you may find yourself back in the depths of despair, replaying an old story in a new place, with new players.

In order to forgive others, you don't necessarily have to be in contact with them. In some cases, this may be for the best. For the Day 19 Practice I ask that you do a forgiveness mediation:

- Find a quiet place that you can concentrate undisturbed for 30 minutes.
- Begin by focusing on your breathing with your eyes closed.
- Feel your body relaxing.
- Feel the life-giving energy of oxygen filling your entire vessel, each cell.
- Once you feel relaxed and comfortable in your mind, replay one of the detrimental scenes of your life.
- Allow yourself to feel the pain, allow yourself to feel the fear, allow yourself to feel the frustration, and allow yourself to feel the anger.
- Allow yourself the space and opportunity to be vulnerable enough and open enough to really feel everything.

You are loved beyond measure and beautiful beyond words. All your angels, guardians, and guides are with you! As you begin this inner work of healing, God Herself smiles down on you, sending you loving rays of rejuvenation.

- While experiencing your visualization, ask the person why he/she did whatever it was to you.
- Allow space for an answer.
- See if you can have a back-and-forth conversation in this space, in which you are able to communicate to the person how you felt exactly and how that experience has impacted your life.
- Allow space for answers.

Get out of your conscious mind and just allow this process to happen.

- At the end of your conversation, visualize yourself saying, "I forgive you", while looking that person in the eye.
- Envision yourself putting that person and that experience on a boat, now watch that boat sail away into the distance...

Day 20

MAKING A LOVING COMMITMENT TO YOURSELF

I just came back from a visit with one of my soul BFF's. She is an amazing spirit; a shamanic practitioner, reiki master, intuitive power-house, healer, artist, and business owner amongst other things. Due to her large skill set, she tends to stay very busy. We find ourselves in a reoccurring conversation quite often about how the Universe sends her signs and signals to "relax and take a break." Since I've known her, I haven't seen her take a full day all the way off. In my mind, taking a day off means lying around in my pj's all day, ordering food, and binge-watching Netflix shows.

A lot of times when we are being busy bees, attempting to pollinate every flower in The Universe overnight, The Universe must often use a more boisterous method to get us to slow down and rest; we might get sick or even sprain an ankle. Being in tune with Uni means that you are also in tune with your body. Your body will give you very subtle urges; to get some rest, slow down, or to stop eating so much fried food. I know life is happening all the time, but if you're not able to give your best because you are tired, then what are you giving?

My soul BFF (let's call her Sarah) also creates quite exquisite works of art through an innate passion for creation itself. In such, I believe that when she's in that creative zone, which she often is, she can work and work and work.

From my perspective, today marked a very loving milestone in Sarah's life. When we were talking, she said that she made a loving commitment to herself and to her body by committing to do yoga five times per week. When I heard her say that, I got soo excited for her. I know how hard it is for her not to work. My excitement for Sarah stemmed from knowing that she had made a commitment of love to herself. *"For five days a week I am going to focus on my body, my breathing, my mind, and my soul. If I get busy during the week that's fine because now I am setting aside time for me."*

One of my loving commitments to myself is meditation. Meditation has become a cornerstone of who I am and what I do, so much so that it has become a daily practice for me. If I did one thing today, it would be that I meditated. Another one of my loving commitments to myself is going to the gym. Through intimate inner work, I have built a special bond with my body, and as a result of this bond, I have discovered a new realm of being where my body and soul communicate with one another clearly and effortlessly.

My body gently tells me what it needs, what it likes, and what it dislikes. Being active is one of the things my body happens to like, therefore, I work out approximately five days per week. If I don't go to the gym and I don't meditate, I turn into a gremlin. My emotional resonance isn't as streamlined when I don't meditate and/or workout, as I lack my usual internal Zen-like focus. Since I really like being happy and I also like to give the best part of me to everyone I meet, I must adhere to the loving commitments that I have made to myself. If I am constantly at my best, then I can constantly give my best.

***

You matter.

***

That is why making one or more loving commitments to yourself is important on your journey to inner peace. If you constantly overlook your needs, instead giving your attention to your career, or your partner, or your family, or friends, then you are constantly overlooking You. If you are constantly overlooking You, then you will also be constantly overlooking what You need. If you are always overlooking what You need, then You are always going without what You need. How can you possibly give your best to the people around you if you are constantly operating from a place where you are without that which you need to fully be yourself?

If your car is always out of gas, where is it that you might go? How can you give energy, if you have no energy to give? What replenishes your soul? Making a loving commitment to yourself means that you make a commitment to do something at least once per week that replenishes your soul, something that benefits the overall being called You.

You can commit to something as small as eating one piece of organic fruit per week. You can commit to going to the gym once per week; working out releases endorphins so you'll be happier during the day each day you do work out. You can commit to meditating five minutes per day. Pick something that will be easy to commit to. Small acts of love built up over the course of a year can have profound and monumental impacts on your life.

The Day 20 Practice asks that you find something that rejuvenates your soul and commit to doing it so as to make a habit out of it. We want to make peace, happiness, love, and understanding habitual. Peace should be our default setting, the resonance we always return to no matter the circumstances of our life, but for this to be accomplished our soul/spirit must be electrified.

To electrify your soul, simply give it love. Making a commitment to give love to yourself means that you are also making a commitment to give peace to yourself; one rock, two stones. The more love you have to offer, the more peace you will receive. Making a commitment to yourself will be an act of love that will result in a state of inner peace.

Day 21

BEFRIENDING THE NEGATIVE MIND

Driving home one night, I found myself in a conversation with...myself, per the usual. Thinking about the new life I found myself being reborn into propelled feelings of bliss throughout my entire being. A big smile confiscated my entire face as gratitude and joy filled my soul. I had finally come to the point I had been preparing for my entire life. All the ups and downs, the feelings of being lost, the anxiety, the depression, the triumphs, and the setbacks had all finally come together. The realization that *I'm here!* filled my entire being. *My dreams are coming true, and Uni is co-creating this awesomeness with me!*

However, not too long after this upheaval of positivity, my mind as it does, searched out for the one fearful thought it could find, seemingly rummaging through an old file cabinet that had been locked away in some back office of my mind. "Hold on there one second..." as a seemingly different part of me interrupted the love fest of happy thoughts I was having:

"I would like to present document A. 753 and I would like to highlight

subparagraph a.1: What if ______ doesn't happen, and what if you don't get _____? Remember that one time you were excited about______ and it fell through? Don't get your hopes up because it seems as if struggle and challenge are what you will experience the most of in your lifetime. In closing I would also like to ask, what will you do if it doesn't work out the way you think it will?"

I replied to my negative counterpart with, "What is wrong with you?! You're really sick, you know that? You can't just sit back and let us be happy for five minutes, can you?"

I think I may have hurt the negative mind's feeling a bit. Let's call him Ted from here on out to make it easier. Once more, another part of me (Ted) seemed to respond with:

"Yeah but, if it weren't for me, you would probably hurt yourself a lot more, you wouldn't show any restraint, ever, and you would probably be dead by now!"

"Sheesh... emotional much?" I responded from a place of peaceful neutrality.

Of course, Uni had to add some synchronicity to the equation in order to put the proper exclamation point on the message She was trying to convey to me. Later that same night we talked about "The Negative Mind" in my Kundalini Yoga class. We also discussed how Ted was actually a friend, meant to lend a hand in the self-control category of my life. This obviously hit home for me as I had just had a conversation in my head with Ted about the same thing!

Ted (the negative mind) will always be there. Get used to it. But because Ted *will* always be there and since Ted *is* an integral part of our flight or fight and survival instincts, befriending Ted made a whole lot more sense. Ted is like our personal, overly compulsive risk analysis agent. His job is to keep us safe at all costs, so he will constantly make sure that all our decisions are based in some correspondence of rationale. We may, however, experience chronic anxiety in our lives if we let Ted run the show. If you are to reach a place of immovable inner peace, you must not allow your mind to run rampant. You are the CEO and Ted works for you. Make sure Ted knows that.

My new practice has been to literally talk to Ted whenever he gets a little too worried or frantic. In my mind, I visualize myself sitting down with Ted and I listen intently to what he has to say from a loving perceptive. I tell him that I understand him, I question his stance, and I lovingly communicate my position to him.

Most often, I can get my point across as well as calm Ted down by listing all the occurrences when things happened in my favor due to some unperceived outside force of Divinity. God has, without a doubt, shown me Her presence time and time again without fail. When things could have gone south for me on many different occasions, a loving hand would always come down from out of nowhere and deliver me. Even Ted cannot deny Uni's presence in my life, so when I do remind Ted of the times The Universe came to bat for me, he humbly agrees and retracts most of his anxious inquiries.

One of the reasons I propagate such a peaceful stance in my life is that I can engage The Negative Mind, aka Ted, with love and understanding. When we ignore something, it becomes bigger. When we give our attention to our fears, we shed light on them, and where there is light, there is love and healing. Love and attention are synonymous with one another.

It helps greatly to act as if the negative mind talk you experience is coming from a child within you who feels alone and afraid; give that part of you a name. Listen to his/her interjections. Try to understand the logic behind his/her anxious speculations. If you can make peace with all aspects of yourself, then you will undoubtedly become more peaceful. If you make an enemy out of any part of yourself, then you will forever be at war.

When you shift your perspective and are able to seek the opportunities to grow in each and every instance of vexation, then everything in your life will become a gift. If God is omnipresent, then God must be hiding somewhere in The Negative Mind as well. If you can find where God is, even in the seeming negative, then your entire life will become your biggest miracle.

The Day 21 Practice asks that you start to develop a relationship with The Negative Mind. Give it a name, dissect its rationale, question its judgment. See The Negative Mind as a child, or even the child version of you who may feel lost and alone. All thoughts imbued in love are from God, and if the thoughts are not imbued in love, they come forth from another source; let this be your compass.

Traumas happen to us all throughout life. These traumas may never be healed and may cause us to become anxious, fearful, or depressed later in life. From this place of anxious fearfulness that the unhealed parts of us endure, come thoughts saturated in trepidation. In order to heal The Negative Mind, we must get to the bottom of why we have certain recurring negative thoughts. In order to do this we must develop a relationship with this not so savory part of ourselves in order to heal.

Day 22

THE CROSSWALK SAYS, "WALK."

When you have big dreams or aspirations, it is easy to become discouraged even before you start your journey. You look ahead and see a winding trail that vanishes into thick vegetation. Your trail guide points vaguely to the top of ice-capped peaks and says, "We'll be camping up there the fifth night at 15,000 ft." A reluctant ambiguity fills your essence as you begin to ponder just how hard and how long getting to this mountain top will actually be. Your mind happily proposes a rational excuse, "Maybe I'll just go in the springtime instead when there's not so much ice. Yeah, honestly, spring sounds a lot better. Nicer weather, flowers in bloom, and butterflies bouncing through the air."

Spring comes around, you are about to begin your journey for the second time, and once more the same apprehension comes over you as you look at the remote mountain peaks that seem like they're a lifetime away. "Hiking shoes, I need better hiking shoes. Plus, it's not as warm as I thought it would be this time of year and I haven't seen a single butterfly today yet either. When it warms up and I get new hiking boots and there are more butterflies out and about, then I will go for sure."

Summer comes with an encore of reluctance as you come up with yet another rational excuse as to why you simply cannot start the seemingly infinite journey to the mountain top. In our human being-ness it is quite easy to wait for conditions to be perfect in order for us to start; a new business, working out, dieting, or embarking on the journey to our dreams. Fear accompanied with laziness is the perfect breeding ground for unfulfilling contentment.

We make excuses as to why we can't accomplish our dreams, using the "not having the ideal conditions for flight" as a crutch. But if we really wanted to get there, we would start walking if need be. What happens as a result of this continued delay of takeoff is that life flashes by and before we know it, it's over, and our dreams are left in the intangible realm.

I read this very cool and interesting book about what we experience after death, "Consciousness Beyond Life: The Science of Near Death Experience", by Dr. Pim van Lommel. One of the most intriguing topics covered in his book was that of a life review.

In our life review we are shown all the times where we gave love, and then we experience the exact feelings that we gave to the other person. We are also shown the repercussions of all the times when we gave anger, fear, or negativity, and once more we experience the exact feelings those on the receiving end endured. In both cases, we are enabled to feel exactly how the other person felt as a result of what we decided to offer them. As our life review continues, we are also shown all the opportunities that we passed up, as well as what our lives could have been if we had acted upon those opportunities.

I couldn't imagine sitting there and being shown a scene of me living my dream life as a result of taking that leap I was too fearful or doubtful to take. I now understand that I have so much creativity, love, passion, and magic inside of me, and I also have the faith and innate belief that I can turn my highest intangible thoughts into reality.

To turn my highest intangible thoughts into reality, I must constantly walk through my fears of failure, my fears of rejection, all my doubts, procrastination, and of course, Ted's poetic contentions. Every day I am challenged to overcome those things. When I look at what is right in front of me and what I can accomplish today with the resources I have at hand, I hit the ball out of the park every time. When I look too far into the future, attempting to effectively plot out my course, even though I don't know all the factors or have all the information, I can become un-centered; this place of imbalance equates to dispiritedness. But, I have found that if I do what I can do today, when it comes to my goals and aspirations, then I open up the floodgates for Uni's energy to work with and through me.

The Universe wants the absolute best for you and is waiting with countless truckloads of miracles and blessings for you at your front gate of commitment. To let God in, you just have to buzz the front gate. To buzz the front gate, you must do the work.

If you want to lose weight but right now you can't afford a gym membership or personal trainer, look up workouts and start doing what you can at home. If you want to eat healthier but going organic doesn't agree with your financial situation, try eating one piece of organic fruit per day. If you want to start your own company but you don't have the financial backing right now, try selling your products on a small scale.

One of the most significant quotes I have heard on my personal journey to inner peace is, ***"If you won't do it when it's hard, then you won't do it when it's easy."*** If you can do the work with limited resources when conditions aren't perfect, imagine what you could accomplish when you do have the resources and when everything seemingly lines up for you; you'll be a powerhouse!

I want to stress the importance of doing the work because, when you do really settle in and go for it, even if you don't have all the supplies, all the time, or all the necessary materials, the magic of Heaven will leap in to assist you and you will begin to see God tangibly working in your life. Miracles will be commonplace for you. It will seem as if you want/need a thing and from unexpected channels it will appear on your doorstep. Your partnership in cultivating your dreams will be a 50/50 split with The Universe, but you have to do what you can right now in regard to getting to that mountain top of yours, in order for Uni to fully assist you.

***

"Take one step and the gods will take ten for you..."~Joseph Campbell

***

The Day 22 Practice asks you to stop waiting. Do something small or do something big as often as you can to get to your mountain top; the key is simply to do something and to remain consistent. Don't let life pass you by. Don't be a caterpillar who never spun a cocoon. As you view your progress on your journey because of your consistency, you will be filled with gratitude, appreciation, and a sense of self-pride. Through the combination of these feelings and your conscious efforts to bring the intangible to the tangible, you will be filled with more happiness and thereby, more peace.

Day 23

⨯⨯⨯

CLEANLINESS IS NEXT TO GODLINESS

I've touched on the aspect of flow and how it correlates to the workings of The Universe multiple times throughout this guidebook. The identification of flow as a crucial component in the way you perceive the energy of God is critical because it is through this perception and your ability to incorporate this aspect of flow into your daily life, that you will find a more peaceful progression through all your endeavors.

The human body uses flow as a means of properly nurturing all the systems of the body. Oxygen, key vitamins, and nutrients are transferred throughout the body via the circulatory system. Disease may manifest itself as a result of blockages in this system of flow. Heart Disease is the number one cause of death in the world. Heart Disease results from a blockage of the arteries due to plaque buildup. Here, the apparent correlation between the blockage of flow and decadence is easily illustrated.

Peace is an aftereffect of the tranquility in which internal energy exhibits itself outwardly. When we hold onto anger, we block the energetic flow of peace; the results of this will be constriction, always. If we allow the anger to flow through us *without acting out* from a place of anger, we can open the valve that allows love to flow through instead. Where there is love, there is healing. When you can look for blockages in any aspect of your life, you will begin to disentangle those areas and allow love and therefore, healing to properly flow through you.

Our external world is but a reflection of our internal world. If we look outwardly and see disorganization and disorder, we can come to understand that our internal mindset and resonance must be synonymous. When I made the decision to make organization and cleanliness in my external world a priority, I experienced an immediate transformation internally; I felt lighter. The lighter I felt, the happier I felt. The happier I felt, the more at peace I began to feel.

I previously resided in Los Angeles, California. When I first moved to LA, I was in a small space that was by no means the Ritz Carlton. I always envisioned myself being in a home of my own, filled with love and light that reflected my own unique energy. I was gifted with the time and space to evolve significantly on my spiritual journey during my time in LA and in my small room I began to practice the art of flow.

I believe I was able to fast track my progress to that which I yearned for externally by setting the stage for it, "already being there." I felt a strong urge to begin to treat my small space with more love, cleaning and organizing it as much as possible.

Before, I had the attitude of, "when I move into a bigger, better place, then I will organize more, clean more, and hang up cool art that reflects my vibe." Even though I wanted to be somewhere else, for the first time I had to really accept where I was whole-heartedly, and thus I began to treat my small space like the house of my dreams.

As I began to organize my space by filing away papers, getting rid of things which I no longer needed, and always making sure my room was clean and the bed made, the magic began to happen. Before I knew it, a very swift succession of events resulted in moving into a larger, more comfortable residence.

Introduction to Feng Shui

Feng Shui is a Chinese method of energetic harmonization through the particular placement of objects in a given space – whether that be the home or garden – resulting in good fortune and/or prosperity. Feng Shui's literal translation is "wind, water." In eastern cultures, the idea of flow and how it pertains to ultimate happiness is of key importance. If you would like more peace, more happiness, more joy, or more love, begin by facilitating the prime conditions that will allow for flow in your external life. You can do this by beginning to clean and organize your space.

- Organize and clean the spaces where you spend the predominate amount of time.
- Try to clean the interior and exterior of your car as much as possible.
- Begin to organize and file any important papers or documents in alphabetical order so you can find them with ease.
- **Make your bed every day.**
- Make sure the dishes are cleaned and put away neatly each day (or as much as possible).
- If you live with a partner, family member, or roommate, you can even assign different areas of the house for someone to be the "Flow Manager" of. Someone could be in charge of the energetic flow of the kitchen, while another person could be in charge of the energetic flow of the bathroom.
- If you live with other people and they don't seem to be too concerned with your new practice of tidiness, just try to make sure that your room/space is as cleaned and organized as possible.

An aftereffect of practicing the art of flow, or Feng Shui, is that you will begin to pick up on the subtle energies around you. As you are able to sense those subtle energies more and more, you will be able to clean up any disharmonies you feel externally at once. Usually, what happens is that these "dis-harmonic" blockages subtly add up over time and are then experienced as some sort of more drastic tribulation.

Nature, The Universe, and life itself are in a constant state of evolution. This evolutionary process to betterment happens gradually. The opposite is true as well; adversity rarely occurs as a result of an instantaneous transformation, but manifests as a result of a buildup. If you can become aware of the small disturbances in the energetic field around you as soon as they occur, then you will immediately be able to nip them in the bud, before they blossom.

Think of your life as an infinite highway that leads to successive manifestations of fulfillment and joy. When things are disorganized, dirty, and unkempt, bumper to bumper traffic fills this highway. When things are organized, clean, neat, and orderly, not a single car is on the road. On the way to the continued fulfillment of your dreams would you rather have gridlocked traffic or open roads as far as the eye can see?

The Day 23 Practice asks that you begin to organize your life. Keep things neat and tidy. Make your bed every morning. Do an internet search on Feng Shui or buy a book on the topic. This is an attempt to sensitize your feelers. What I mean by that is, practicing Feng Shui will assist you in feeling the energy of your personal space, so that when the energy of that space is off, you will know exactly how to fix it, either by moving something around, cleaning, or organizing. This practice in your home will then translate to your spirit world, as well as the world at large; when the energy is off in a place or within yourself, you will know and feel it immediately. You will also know what to do to fix the disturbance, maybe by taking a few deep breaths or offering some words of encouragement.

May your life reflect flow both internally and externally, so that you may live in tune with the rhythm of The Universe. Life can become one big dance party once you get on beat.

Day 24

LET'S PRETEND TO BE LITTLE SUNS

Let's pretend that you are a being made of pure energy and light (which you are). Let's also go as far as saying that you are made entirely of photons, i.e., light energy. In this illustration, you are basically like a little sun. Just like the actual sun, wherever you place your attention/ give your energy/send your light, growth occurs.

So, if you place your attention on the injustices of the world, on the things you regret, or on the issues that cause you to worry...those things will grow. This also means that if you place your attention on the things that you love, the aspects of life that you are grateful for, as well as all the people, opportunities, and experiences that fill you with love, those things will grow as well. So, while pretending to be a little sun, what is it that you would like to grow in the next moments of your life?

Imagine living each day from the mindset of "I am a little sun, and whatever I focus on grows!" When you are constantly shedding your light on the things which you love, you are constantly feeling the energy of love. If you are constantly feeling the energy of love, then you will only be able to give what you are constantly feeling, which is love. If you come to the point where you are only able to give love, then you will also reach the point where all that you receive is love. Envision what your life might resemble if the only thing you ever received was love. Can you conceive of a world where all people only gave and therefore received love?

The path of continued enlightenment and peace comes as a result of successive evolutionary advancements in perspective. If you can constantly look for the good, you will constantly grow the good, making your entire life...good. Coming forth in all your endeavors from the stance of "I am a little sun" will empower you. Instead of feeling like a victim to circumstances outside of your control, you could shine your light on whatever you would like to see grow.

During challenging experiences, you could ask yourself, "What is my current perspective?" The act of pausing and then questioning will center you in the present moment. From this place of centeredness, you will experience the essence of peace as an assistant. The benefit of making a decision in the presence of peace results in a more controlled response. Instead of simply *reacting*, you will make a conscious choice as to where you want to come from as a response to this external stimuli. Believing that you are a little sun will allow you to act as such and focus your light wherever you believe may be of greatest benefit to you.

No matter how bad things may appear to be on the surface, almost any situation will have some underlying positive aspect. Amid illness or divorce, imagine the transformative abilities you may use by highlighting whatever small amount of good you can find in the situation. You do not have to necessarily ignore the "negative" aspects; however, giving more of your energy to the positive aspects can expedite healing and happiness.

Pretending to be little suns works wonders if you find yourself in a perceived "low point" in your life. By simply shining your light/ giving your attention to whatever good you can find, you will begin to eventually feel lighter and therefore happier. Remember, the process towards infinite enrichment always happens little by little; no rose ever blossomed overnight.

As you continue to fill your vessel with happy lightness, eventually, like a plant needing to be repotted because it needs more space, The Universe will happily drop in to replant you in a much bigger, better container.

The Day 24 Practice asks that, before you leave your house in the morning affirm, "I am a little sun and whatever I place my attention on grows." This way during the day when your mind wanders off down the path of anxiety or fear, you can immediately course correct by shifting your focus to something that you're grateful for, that you love, or that makes you happy. Try to use this affirmation throughout the day as well, as a reminder.

Day 25

THE BREATH WORKS
HEALING SPA

For the Day 25 Practice I ask that you get a membership to The Breath Works Healing Spa and make the commitment of checking in at least once per day. What I mean by this is that, each day you make a commitment to pausing and focusing on your breath.

We previously discussed the sympathetic nervous system and its relationship to our fight or flight response during Day 2 of this 30 Day Practice. When activated, the sympathetic nervous system sends oxygen to the arms and legs, increases the heart rate, dilates the pupils, and releases adrenaline, all in hopes of keeping us alive from imminent death. In addition, the stimulation of the sympathetic nervous system sends out less oxygen to the prefrontal cortex, which is responsible for rational clear thinking.

By contrast, when activated, the parasympathetic nervous system decreases the heart rate and respiratory activity, as well as relaxes the muscles. The parasympathetic nervous system essentially annuls the work of the sympathetic nervous system; it relaxes the body. Now, guess how we can activate the parasympathetic nervous system, thereby calming our entire body? Through deep breathing.

Anytime you pause and focus on the gentle rhythm of the breath, you root yourself in the present moment; you calm down. It is in this present moment, and only in this moment that life is happening. It is also in this present moment that you are okay. You may have an appointment for surgery tomorrow, or a court date next month that may saturate you with fear and anxiety, but right now, in this moment, everything is okay. Your breath will remind your body and therefore your mind of this.

The act of pausing is a powerful demonstration of faith. To be able to stop in a world that constantly demands that you go, reflects an internal disposition that is sure of oneness with God.

If I am aware that I am perfectly safe right now, and if I am aware that the gift of life, through my breathing, is given to me in infinite abundance, then I must be loved by a higher power. My breathing, therefore, my existence, is proof of The Universe's love for me.

Through the act of pausing and focusing on the breath, you will realize that your essential needs are constantly being met through the copious flow of life-giving oxygen. You need not seek out the air you breathe, as it is steadily supplied to you, infinitely awaiting your beckoning call.

The breath at the foundation of life is forever yours, and without it you can have neither challenge nor triumph. Without it you cannot move, talk, dance, write, walk, sing, love, or be. God whispers with each breath, "What you need is always supplied." This promise gives birth to trust. *Consider the lilies and how they toil not or spin not.* If God's love extends to a plant in such a way that all its needs simply rain down upon it, do you figure that His love would not deliver your needs to your doorstep as well? Do you believe that you are separate from nature? Finding yourself in creation and as a member of creation, is it sane to think that God's love can miss you? If you are not separate from God, then even within this challenge or that hardship, God is there with you, around you, within you.

The magic of love is on full display each time you breathe. The by-product of each exhale (carbon dioxide) feeds and nourishes all plant life. As you exhale the plants and trees of the world inhale, and as you inhale so, too, do they exhale. You are a part of a naturally perfect rhythmic process. You matter, and your wellbeing and safety matter. When you feel out of sorts, worried, off balance, fearful, or anxious, pause and focus on your breath. As you inhale, know that you are an integral part of creation, just like a necessary component of an engine. This Universe works because you are here, now, being, breathing.

In our human-doing-ness, rushing here or there, checking off items on our to-do lists, meeting people, clocking in, clocking out, planning the future, and going to the grocery store, it is easy to get consumed with our thoughts, to forget about our true home, the present moment.

Home is where we feel connected to the entire Universe. When we are home, we are consciously aware that we are a part of the whole. Contrarily, when we are busily living our lives, we may believe that we are apart from the whole. In this place of apparent separation, we may experience suffering. Feeling alone, we may make a decision as if we are alone. Decisions based in false perceptions will result in dissonance.

The path to peace is perhaps the most challenging path your soul will endeavor to traverse. Your breath, however, is a loyal ally in this holy pursuit of pursuits. When you pause and focus on the breath, you root yourself in the now. The more you exercise your presence in the present, the further you will extend your roots. The deeper your roots, the more solidity you will exhibit as you begin to stand taller and firmer.

***

If the most basic requirement for your heart to beat is constantly gifted to you, then what possibly would have been created that was meant to sabotage you?

***

The Day 25 Practice asks that you make an effort to do this daily breathing exercise:

- Breathing in, know that this breath is a gift from Source.
- Breathing out, give appreciation for the love that is constantly supplied to you.
- Breathing in, feel light entering each one of your cells.
- Breathing out, see darkness and waste leaving each one of your cells.

The more you check in with your breath during the day, the more at peace you will begin to feel. As you continue with this exercise, you will continue to take steps in the direction of eternal peace.

Day 26

GENTLE PERSISTENCE

Although highly debated, the general scientific consensus is that the Grand Canyon was formed as a result of erosion from the Colorado River five to six million years ago.

If water has the ability to carve through rock, even given a lofty length of time, imagine what you can accomplish as a result of a constant un-satiating search for peace. Imagine what will become of those seemingly impermeable challenges that are cast onto your path. With Love as your accomplice, you will gently wear away at the bedrock that makes up your next mountain.

Even with the faith of a mustard seed, one can move mountains, but you need not move a mountain, as your peace will enable you to cut directly through it. Just like the winding Colorado River, you can also mold an entirely new world bit by bit. Every instance that you offer peace in the face of adversary, a bit of once-apparent, unmovable rock is taken downriver.

Each occurrence that you command peace, however brief or seemingly trivial, will add a drop of water to a bucket. If a 20-gallon container is left under a modestly leaking faucet without being moved, over time that container will overflow. Each time you find yourself pausing instead of reacting, each time you make a conscious effort to focus on your breath, and each time you decide to choose a loving thought over a fearful thought, you will be adding one drop of water to your container. Your journey to inner peace can be reflected by this container and faucet analogy. When you first set your gaze upon this vastly empty container, you may become discouraged but, "the journey of a thousand miles begins with one step."~Lao Tzu

Though gentle, persistent water (a liquid), has the ability to cut through rock (a solid), something soft has the ability to cut through something hard; I believe nature to be one of the most profound teachers of life. The example of the Grand Canyon is a beautiful illustration of what one can accomplish through steadfastness.

Come from a perspective of "The time it takes for me to reach my destination does not matter because, it is through taking that first step that my destiny is assured. It is only through the cessation of my steps that I may come to experience failure." Even if "failure" happens, know that failure is a temporary state, only relating to non-movement. If you truly believe the aforementioned, you will surely follow the example of The Colorado River, and you will experience profound and beautiful transformations in your life.

Don't be concerned with the length of time it takes you to reach your ultimate destination. Taking another example from nature's lesson plan, I would like to mention the metamorphic experience of a caterpillar. Humans have the free-will ability to choose to embody their absolute highest state or not. Nature does not possess such privileges. A honeybee is programmed to pollinate flowers. It is through this process of pollination that more plant life is born. If the honeybee possessed the free-will ability to "change careers", perhaps flowers wouldn't get pollinated, creating a domino effect that would ultimately result in the cataclysmic secession of all animal life on the planet. Like the honey-bee, caterpillars also lack the volition to follow a different path. A caterpillar must become a butterfly, it is a requirement set forth by its natural life process. But imagine the thoughts a caterpillar may have on its journey to becoming a butterfly. Picture the possible fear and uncertainty experienced on his/her path:

"I've been a caterpillar for far too long and all my friends have left the ground, living in the sky, drinking sweet nectar in places that I could only dream of. Am I perhaps not a butterfly at all, but a very small snake and that is why I haven't transformed yet? Maybe I'm just not worthy enough to become a butterfly. Maybe I am not as special as the others. Maybe the magic that I believe in is only a dream..."

Just like the caterpillar, you are ultimately a butterfly. The only thing that can change your destiny is your thoughts about this. You have the free will capability to accept or deny your holy divinity. You will never be forced to live your highest truth. We are endowed with this ability to **choose** to be God, because it is only through the freedom given in this choice that our highest truth can be experienced as such. You need only trust that you are a butterfly in order to transform. The work that you must do is the same work that a river does if it is determined to cut through rock. You must decide not to decide anything else but success. If you persist, you will command miracles.

Practice peace little by little, step by step. Cast away any notion of being anything other than the embodiment of peace. If you can seek ease in the presence of turmoil, eventually you will wear down all your difficulties until only a picturesque backdrop remains.

The Day 26 Practice asks for your persistence, even when it seems like your challenges are immovable. Your stubbornness will assure your victory. Make a choice not to choose any other outcome but fulfillment. If water can cut through rock....

Day 27

THE REASON YOU CAME HERE...

Imagine that your home is at-one-ment with The Universe, in what many people have referred to as Heaven. In this celestial ream of all-encompassing love and joyfully exuberant abundance, pain, strife, and suffering do not exist. You eternally dwell in this place. Now, imagine spending such a long time in this place that the joy, love, peace, happiness, and absolute tranquility that you experience all becomes a little mundane.

You've been in paradise so long that your soul has started to become antsy; perhaps somewhere in the Garden, the wanderlust bug has bitten you. Your soul begins to crave excitement and some oh-so-juicy drama. Being at peace is wonderful, but adventure seems to be adamantly beckoning your spirit, so you go to God with a proposition...

"I want to feel alive! I want to feel excited! I want to feel thrilled because I am surprised! I want to not know and then find out! Being here with you is amazing but it just feels like there's much more I can experience...like the feeling of fear. I know I am forever at one with you, and I know there is

nothing that could ever really hurt me because of this, but I need a thrill! Is there anything you can think of that we could do?"

The Creator replies, *"Well my child, let's see...What we could do is create a sort of playground for you. Together we could set up a bunch of obstacles and rides. We could also come up with some games you could play there. Ironically, you're not the only one who came to me today with this same feeling. It seems that a lot of your brothers and sisters are asking for the same things you are. So, I have decided to make one big playground where all of you can play together. We can set the stage for this playground and really go over every minute detail about what will happen there, then we can make it so you forget all about me and all about here; I think because of the 'amnesia'''you'll really get that excitement you're seeking. Don't worry though, even with this, 'forgetting', you will still be tethered to me. I will build a transmitter, we'll call it 'intuition' that I will put within your soul that can feel me and hear me at all times; that way if you get too forgetful, or too worried, or if you feel lost, or you get too caught up in the seeming realness of the playground, you can just call me up. How's that sound?"*

You are amazed *"Wowweee!! That sounds so cool! I also like the fact that all my brothers and sisters will be there too. This is going to be fun! Will I recognize them? Will they have forgotten, too? This all sounds exactly like what I want. How did you think of this so fast!?"*

Her belly laugh is deep, *"Hahaha. I love your enthusiasm! The transmitter/intuition that I will equip you with will also help you recognize your family. They will all have amnesia, too, but they will all be equipped with their very own transmitters as well. Now, this trip will be challenging because you won't really remember who you are, but that is one of the main reasons why things will be so interestingly thrilling. What we can also do is make a list of, let's say, 100 events that you must have no matter what. The other events in your life will be experienced as a result of the choices that you make on the playground; we will call it...'cause and effect.' Cause and effect will be a tool that you can use to help you 'win' the game. To 'win' the playground game, all you have to do is return home. This will be extremely challenging because you won't really know how to get back here. The transmitter, along with cause and effect, will guide you but returning home is ultimately up to you."*

You think before replying, *"Hmm...I don't know how, even with this 'amnesia' thing, it will be hard to make it back home. I mean, this is what/ who I am. I think even if I forget, I will somehow remember. This whole thing sounds very interesting. I like the fact that there will be 100 events that we get to pick out together that I must experience. I feel like I will always be reminded of home, at least during those 100 times. Lol. So, I get this transmitter thingy called intuition, there's this thing called 'cause and effect', and my brothers and sisters will be there. How can I not win this game? Let's do it!"*

With the stage set and the pre-opt amnesia administered, you journey down to what is called the third Dimension, on the playground God made for you called 'Earth.' You find yourself here, now, reading this book. What if this story were true and not only are you related to all other humans on a soul level, but you also have a transmitter God installed within your soul, and there were 100 events that you would have to experience no matter what? How would you behave if you knew that the next challenge in your life was something you picked, lovingly created to assist you on your journey home, there to help you remember who you truly were?

I thought about this myself and I felt empowered and excited. If Uni and I had sat down together in the realm of perfect harmony and thoughtfully planned out 100 events that would challenge, thrill, and transform me, all in hopes of bringing me back to a realm of perfect harmony, I would embrace every challenge, trial, tribulation, and setback, knowing that I was more than equipped to handle each one of them. If God and I planned all of this out, in order to help me realize my one-ness with Him in the Kingdom of Heaven, all the while giving my soul a thrilling vacation from perfection, then bring it! Bring it all. Bring on the good, the bad, the mundane, and the unusual.

Living life as if God created every challenging instance in your life, with you at the table as co-creator, can radically empower you. As a result of our amnesia, we see separation as a truth. It is this illusion that causes us suffering in that we may feel alone, especially in our darkest hours. When things seem in disarray, we may feel as if we have made a mistake or that we're off course somehow. But what if we came to every uncomfortable situation that we may be faced with as though we planned it out so that we could remember who we really were?

The harvest of faith is success. Faith can move mountains because it is through a belief that the mountain can be moved, that one may attempt to move it. If you believe that you are alone, your causes and therefore your effects will be in correlation with your idea of separation. If you believe that you are the co-creator of everything in your life, you will come forth with a determined audacity whenever adversity knocks at your door.

The Day 27 Practice asks that you believe that there are 100 events in your life that must happen to you in order for you to truly remember and realize your ultimate truth. This attitude will allow you to maintain a peaceful stance even in the face of a storm. If you make this choice right now, the next time life throws you a curveball, your relaxed state of confidence will allow you to hit a game winning, walk-off home run!

Remember back on the hardships of your life. Try to evaluate each one of them thoroughly. Search each one of these instances for potential lessons that they may have offered. See what wisdom you can gain by looking back.

Let your intuition be your guide.

Day 28

FEEL IT ALL

Keeping right along with the Day 27 Practice, remember that your ultimate destiny is assured. The Kingdom of Heaven is you. You are here, now, so that you can have the thrilling experiences of being human, while feeling all the juicy feelings associated with this state, on the road trip back home.

You are here to **feel** the hurt.

You are here to **feel** the uncertainty.

You are here to **feel** the pain.

You are here to **feel** the anxiety.

You are here to **feel** the worry.

You are here to **feel** the happiness.

You are here to **feel** the gratitude.

You are here to **feel** the love.

You are here to **feel** the excitement.

And you are here to **feel** the peace.

The lusciousness of life is available to you through your senses and your feelings. We are meant to feel scared, so that we can experience and feel what security is. The dramatic uncertainty of life is enchanting, gripping, breathtaking, and riveting. Miracles happen the moment all hope is lost. Can you remember a time in your life when something magical happened in your favor that spared you from seeming demise? What did it feel like? How did that act of grace change the way you looked at things?

One of the greatest gifts that we may have been given is this matrix of duality- the contrasting scale of emotions and feelings. An example is, worrying frantically just to have things turn out fine- stress and relief. Experiencing heartbreak can make the next love seem sweeter- pain and joy. It is when we experience struggle that we come to deeply and intimately understand peace.

If you knew everything, life wouldn't be worth living. Nothing would ever excite you or frighten you; in fact, you would be infinitely unmoved, apathetic, and insensitive. You would never feel proud of yourself because there would never be a stage set on which you could display your fortitude. Remember the last time you were scared to do something you knew would benefit you and you did it despite those apprehensive feelings? How did you feel afterwards?

***

"Success is an inside job" ~ *Dr. Wayne Dyer*
***

I don't know what will happen in the next moments of my life. I don't know if my dreams will come true, but I **believe** they will. To see my beliefs come to fruition despite my fearful feelings and doubts gives evidence to something deeper taking place. I don't run away from the feelings of being scared anymore. Instead, I allow those emotions to have a seat at my table. I feel the feeling all the while taking note of the reason it is there. I also make sure and take note of how things previously worked out for me even in the presence of worry.

Life is one big dramatic movie! There are twists and turns, as well as ups and downs that may leave you on the edge of your seat. In some scenes you may barely be able to look at what is taking place as your heart is beating out of your chest from fear. Some scenes will bring tears to your eyes, and some scenes make you want scream at the projection. You will have a much smoother and way more fun time at the movie theater of life if you can constantly remind yourself that you are the co-producer and co-writer of your own movie called life and that Great Spirit is your co-creative partner.

The key to successfully feeling all the feelings without being overwhelmed by them is to continually root yourself in the present moment. Even if there is a severe storm warning in your life and broadcasts say it will be one of the worst storms in history, rooting yourself in the present moment by utilizing your breath will allow you to realize/experience/be the peace you seek. If you can be peaceful in the present, you can be peaceful anywhere, because life is only happening right now.

You are beyond space and time.

You are beyond your thoughts.

You are beyond your feelings.

Your feelings are like the changing currents or the wind, while you are the ocean and the sky.

There were times in the past where I would find myself feeling guilty for feeling worried or fearful because I had read, "The Lord said, Fear thou not; for I am with thee: be not dismayed; for I am thy God: I will strengthen thee; yea, I will help thee; yea, I will uphold thee with the right hand of my righteousness." (Isaiah 41:10) This feeling of guilt was related to what I had heard about God-that He was angry, spiteful, and jealous. I didn't want to get on the bad side of this guy and be reprimanded due to my lack of faith, so I just hid the fact that I was scared from myself, God, and the world.

The continued pushing down of my emotions was very spiritually, emotionally, and physically detrimental to myself, but I didn't want God to be mad at me. Over time all the guilt and fear I had become so accustomed to burying, would eventually come out in an overly dramatic and inappropriate fashion, leaving behind a trail of hurt feelings and charred bridges. Something had to change. I had to acknowledge my feelings so that I could see the truth and gift in why they had presented themselves to me. To feel safe enough to be open and honest, my idea about God had to change.

I previously discussed with you the importance of building a personal relationship with God and how God's relationship with you will be different than Her relationship with anyone else. It is important that you have your very own idea of what God is and how God communicates with you, because you will need to feel loved enough and safe enough to be completely vulnerable with God. It is only through this complete exposure that you will be able to see everything in you that needs to be healed.

Healing can only occur once there is an acknowledgment of disease. The religious ideology of old that paints a picture of a destructive, mean, patriarchal, and vengeful God is not true. In the self-seeking of God, you will find clues all along the trail as to Her true loving nature. Love is stronger than fear, making God's love the strongest force in existence and non-existence. Through your vulnerability with God, you will understand what true love really is. Through your realization of true love, you will find ease in baring your fears and "sins" openly for healing. Through your trust, you will be baptized and born again in Holy Matrimony with All That Is Good.

Feel whatever you are feeling while attempting to stay rooted in your divine unity with Source. Remember, "This is your show!" You can only let fear overwhelm you if you choose to believe that you are alone amid your tribulations. If you believe you are alone, then you believe you are separate. If you believe you are separate, then you must also believe that you are not *a* part of creation.

Interwoven togetherness is at the foundation of our perceived Universe; smaller things make up larger things through atomic, covalent, and ionic bonds. The word bond emphasizes togetherness. Even if it appears that you are alone, you would have to defy the natural order of The Universe in order to make this a truth.

There is a great power in the ability to feel your way through life. My personal experience has shown me that The Universe/All That Is, is energy, and because energy moves via waves, I am in one big ocean. If you can begin to *feel* the subtle changing of the ocean's currents, you can adjust your sails accordingly. As you adjust your sails to coincide with these changes you will find that you experience more of the things you want at a faster rate.

Many of us spend our entire lives tirelessly fighting the changing currents of life, unable to trust the shifting circumstances as a whisper from God; *the portion of my life I spent doing this only resulted in weariness.*

As I venture forth on my path, I can actually *feel* God. In the presence of a perceived fear, I am confident and trusting enough in Uni to allow myself to be vulnerable. Feeling the fear while knowing I am connected to ultimate love and peace is invigorating. Life gets better when you allow yourself to feel everything while knowing and remembering your oneness with God. This is what the Day 28 Practice asks of you.

Day 29

DON'T TAKE IT
PERSONALLY

Someone cuts you off in traffic while screaming a hurtful slur at
you.

Your co-worker always seems to blow things out of proportion and
acts in a passive-aggressive manner towards you.

Your partner displays episodes of jealousy and possessiveness.

You say, "Hi" to a stranger on the street and they don't respond.

A police officer on a power trip pulls you over and acts like a jerk
the whole time.

The people working at the DMV seem aggravated and unmotivated
to assist you.

The list goes on.

Remember, people can only give you what they have to offer. No amount of force will ever extract orange juice from an apple or apple juice from an orange. If someone has spent 20, 30, 40, 50-plus years without searching the caverns of their soul to uncover and heal issues that have transformed malignant hurt into fear, then they will at times give you that fear in the form of anger, agitation, frustration, etc.; that energy must be released somewhere/somehow, and you just so happen to be conveniently in their presence.

Knowing that people may behave in an ill manner towards you because they are hurting deep within themselves can take a huge weight off your shoulders. Their episodes of anger, dishonesty, cruelness, or judgment are all just cries for help. To respond to a cry for help with an attack of your own would be the bigger travesty. Only love can heal fear and pain. No good doctor chastises a patient for yelling and screaming as a result of the pain they are enduring.

Taking others' harshness towards us personally can make us become defensive. When we become defensive, we constrict our energetic fields. As previously discussed, when we constrict the flow of energy, chaos and disruption ensue. If you would like to experience chaos or disruption, I would advise you to become defensive every time someone lashes out at you. If you would like to reach a place of supreme peace, where your tranquility is rooted as deeply as the roots of a thousand-year-old oak tree, I would advise you not to take *anything* personally.

Volcanoes erupt as a result of a buildup of interior pressure. If a person does not have the tools to continually address the increasingly building pressure within themselves, then eventually their lives will erupt. Would you take an erupting volcano's explosiveness personally? If not, then look at your fellow man with the same unattached objectivity.

You should use your intuition to decide when to let things go, and when to stand up for yourself. You have the choice on how to respond to someone's outbursts...with love or with fear. When it comes to personal and intimate relationships, a loving response to fear would be, "______ when you did _____ it really made me feel ______. I really value our relationship, but in order to have a healthy partnership I need you to try not to ______ anymore."

In our close relationships, being lovingly vulnerable disarms the other person and puts the ball in their hands. They will either see the loving space you have created for them as a safe haven, allowing them to open up as well, or they will reject your call to peace. If you continually and consciously come forth with a peaceful openness in response to harshness, yet you are continually and consciously met with fear and anger, this may be a sign to end the relationship. If someone is panicking while drowning, unable to calm down enough to be rescued, the rescuer might be knocked unconscious by a flailing arm and drown themselves. It is not your job to save anyone. Your foremost responsibility will always be to maintain your own well-being, because it is from this place that you will always give your best, most loving energy.

The correct response to fear is love. Placing yourself in the other person's shoes can be advantageous to you as you search for an appropriate response when dealing with an adverse situation. Whenever you can pause before you respond, you are ensuring that you will be coming from a place of rational balance. Responding from a place of rational balance will correspond to a loving solution in most cases. When we react, we commit to suffering. When we respond, we commit to empowerment.

The act of pausing and then responding also opens the space for The Universe to step in and give you some much needed divine perspective. Absolute trust corresponds to pausing, because it is in this "stopping" that you are declaring, "all is well"... and so shall it be. Your energy declares, "I can relax because I know I am supported. I do not need to force a resolution to this situation. I have the faith to wait long enough to allow the resolution to appear."

It is not your job to save the world, but to save the world, you merely need save yourself. I know you can do this because you have already started your journey to sovereignty. You cannot control what other people say or do, but you can control how you respond, what you say, and how you behave. If you wish to see the world happier, more peaceful and more loving, then embody the change you wish to see with every step and every breath you take. Know that another person's anger towards you has little to do with you. Hurt people are likely to hurt other people, because all they have to give is what they have, and all they have is pain.

Additionally, you never know what struggles someone might be enduring on a personal level.

We have each dealt with difficult situations and because of our hardships we may not always come across as joyful. Health issues, loss, financial problems, and traumatic events can make life burdensome. Imagine going through a divorce and a custody battle, while working in a retail environment where you have to be friendly and talk to people. Perhaps, you may be rude on some occasions, and perhaps you may look and feel disconnected at times. Being happy-go-lucky is easy when there are blue skies and sunny days; the challenge is trying to remain optimistic and joyful even when your life seems to be crashing in flames. Giving love as the rebuttal for "negativity" is crucial because your love might just be exactly what that person needs in that particular moment.

The Day 29 Practice asks that you give love as a response to fear, hate, anger, jealousy, rage, or any other form of negativity. The Day 29 Practice does not ask that you allow yourself to be a doormat, however. Use your intuition as a guide to help you determine when it is time to take a firmer stance. You want your love to create a space that allows the other person to feel this opening energetically; by giving love in the face of its opposite, you can immediately calm a situation in most cases. Most often it simply comes down to this: **people just want to be understood**. A lot of people feel alone. A lot of people feel unheard or unrepresented. Love can heal all those issues in an instant.

Day 30

"WHAT SONG AM I SINGING?"

Quick Recap of what "Universe" actually means:

Uni-*prefix*
Definition of *uni-*
:one : single

Verse-*noun*
Definition of *verse-*
1 : a line of metrical writing
metrical writing- "technical writing in the form of poetry, with a
pattern of strong and weak beats." ~idoceonline.com

We can thereby summarize that "Universe" means, one singular beat
or rhythm. Therefore, God singularly vibrates with the essence of peace.

If I asked Uni, "What song are you singing?", she would probably
reply: "Three Little Birds by Bob Marley"; the constant resonation of,
"Every little thing will be alright." The Universe holds the perpetual

vibration of support, love, compassion, healing, understanding, forgiveness, optimism, truth, and of course, peace.

Immovable in His Holy essence, there is nothing else given by God except perfect love and harmony. God can be nothing other than good because God vibrates nothing other than good, the absolute pitch of perfection. There is stillness in the moving waves of the ocean; ebb and flow, in and out, waves reach forth to the shores of man like God reaching for Adam in *The Creation of Adam* by Michelangelo. God will never change Her song, She is always reaching for you; it is through this consistency that your salvation is promised. If we can harmonize with the Holiest of Spirits, then we will become nothing short of gods ourselves and what else should we aim to accomplish in our fleeting existence? Let us be the song of God.

For the Day 30 Practice I ask that you ask yourself each day and, in each moment, as much as possible, especially in those difficult to deal with situations, "What song am I singing?" This question reflects, "What vibrations am I giving?", which reflects, "What energy am I giving?" Because it is through the song that you sing that you will attract the people, experiences, situations, and circumstances that are in harmonic balance with your song.

If you constantly sing "Three Little Birds" by Bob Marley, thereby consistently vibrating, "Every little thing will be alright" well then, every little thing WILL be alright. This is the law of attraction. This is how you WILL manifest everything that you desire; you must get in tune with that which you seek. If you seek peace, sing songs of peace. Feel the vibrations you send out to the world. Your soul cannot speak except through vibration, except through its unique song.

If you can always remember to feel what you are giving, then you will be able to change what you are giving, if need be. If you can change what you are giving in a situation, then you will be able to change what you are receiving in a situation. Constantly asking yourself, "What song am I singing?" means that you are constantly checking in with yourself. You are practicing self-awareness. The more you practice self-awareness, the more your focus will be turned internally. The more you focus on the internal, the greater light you shed on the internal. Where there is light, there is love, and where there is love, there is growth.

Sing your song of love, peace, and harmony so much so that everyone that enters your life either has to start happily dancing on beat, or they will be forced to vacate your presence because they don't like the music. Watch adamantly as things move in and out of your life and know that the changing of your experience is only occurring to match the frequency/vibration/song you are singing.

Remaining consistent in your song of choice will equate to consistency in your experiences of life. Even if things transpire in your life that cause you despair or grief, your congruence to your song will expedite healing. Think of nothing other than your salvation and so it shall be. Give nothing other than peace and peace will be the only thing you receive. Harmonize with The Universe and harmony will be the effect of all your undertakings.

Consistency will be challenging, especially when faced with adversity, yet it is in this place of challenge where you can build the foundations of who you are, what you want, and what you will receive. Words are secondary to sound, sound is secondary to vibration, God does not hear the words you speak, but She feels the vibrations you send Her. She will harmonize with your vibrations, responding based upon what frequency you are emitting. If you sing songs of peace, The Universe will sing songs of peace right along with you. If you sing songs of worry, well then, The Universe will not hesitate to once more, sing along with you. You have the choice in each and every situation to decide what to give/what to sing/how to vibrate. Your vibrations, aka your songs, are your prayers, and The Universe always answers in perfect harmony to what you ask. This is why in many Law of Attraction practices, the lessons are about *feeling* how you wish to feel, not the actual things you wish to obtain.

Decide today who wish to be. Decide today what you wish to have. *Feel* what it feels like to be the highest version of yourself. *Feel* what it feels like to have your grandest dreams come true. Now sing that song everywhere you go. Sing the song that is you. Vibrate the song that is you. As you give so shall you receive. Check in with yourself throughout the day asking, "What song am I singing?" Every night before you go to bed, once more check in with yourself and ask, "What song did I sing today?" Your devotion to the consistency of your song will determine the quality of life that you live.

About The Author...

Proudly hailing from Chicago, Illinois, Jared Madison currently resides in the peaceful Sea Island's, of Beaufort, South Carolina; the place where he happily calls home.

Jared considers himself a "new renaissance man" as his hobbies and interests are diverse. From traveling the world to studying Reiki, Jared also finds solace in the study of quantum physics, cell development and genetics as well as holistic approaches to maintaining optimal health.

In addition to being a business entrepreneur in the field of retail fashion and design, Jared also takes pride in being one of three contributing writers for *Lowcountry Weekly,* a bi-weekly magazine publication where he writes for the Wholly Holistic column.

Jared finds peace and encouragement in the presence of his closest allies and support system in his mother Susan Madison, father Richard Madison, fiancé Kanani Robinson, and his cat "momma-kitty."

For more content follow Jared on TikTok, Instagram, and Facebook **@themagicalminute** where you will find minute long clips of inspiration, motivation, spiritual advice, and wisdom. To listen to his podcast, visit the website, **www.dialingthedivine.com.** Jared also has an upcoming podcast/YouTube show with his mother Susan Madison titled, *The Elephant in The Room;* a mother and son podcast discussing the uncomfortable, problematic and controversial cultural issues of the times.

For any further inquiries email: info@theinnovallc.com